T0346406

The Most Land, the Best Cattle

The Most Land, the Best Cattle

The Waggoners of Texas

Judy Alter

TWODOT®

GUILFORD, CONNECTICUT
HELENA, MONTANA

A · TWODOT® · BOOK

An imprint of Globe Pequot, the trade division of
The Rowman & Littlefield Publishing Group, Inc.
4501 Forbes Blvd., Ste. 200
Lanham, MD 20706
www.rowman.com

Distributed by NATIONAL BOOK NETWORK

British Library Cataloguing in Publication Information available

Library of Congress Cataloging-in-Publication Data

Names: Alter, Judy, 1938- author.
Title: The most land, the best cattle : the Waggoners of Texas / Judy
   Alter.
Other titles: Waggoners of Texas
Description: Helena, Montana : Two Dot, [2021] | Includes bibliographical
   refrerences. | Identifiers: LCCN 2021009796 (print) | LCCN 2021009797 (ebook) | ISBN
   9781493052639 (cloth) | ISBN 9781493052646 (epub)
Subjects: LCSH: Wagner family. | W.T. Waggoner Ranch (Tex.) |
   Ranchers—Texas—Biography. | Texas—Genealogy.
Classification: LCC CS71.W134 2021 (print) | LCC CS71.W134 (ebook) | DDC
   929.20973—dc23
LC record available at https://lccn.loc.gov/2021009796
LC ebook record available at https://lccn.loc.gov/2021009797

♾™ The paper used in this publication meets the minimum requirements of American National Standard for Information Sciences—Permanence of Paper for Printed Library Materials, ANSI/ NISO Z39.48-1992.

Contents

Prologue

IN THE EARLY 1980S, I SPENT A COUPLE OF DAYS AT SANTA Rosa, the home of Electra Waggoner Biggs, on the Waggoner Three D Ranch in North Texas. I don't remember how I wrangled the invitation, but I know I went because I was interested in her as a sculptor. She was, in my eyes, a classic case of an heiress who could have spent her days reading *Silver Screen* and eating bonbons but instead developed her art and career. I went expecting to find evidence of her life as an artist.

Instead, I found an international celebrity, an heiress, and a sculptor—in that order of priorities. Electra was also a widow, mother of two daughters, and grandmother of four. But glimpses of those areas of her life rarely came up except for references to her husband, the late John Biggs. Her daughters did—and still do—keep a much lower profile than earlier generations of their colorful family.

My memories of the visit have grown foggy over the years. I remember being served raspberries and an elegant continental breakfast at a glass-topped table in a small solarium. Mrs. Biggs was preparing for a big dinner party, which meant she and her cook did a trial run, preparing a test of every dish they would serve. I think I benefited from that, but I don't remember any one dish. In *Dining with the Cattle Barons*, the late Sarah Morgan told us Imperial Goulash was one of Mrs. Biggs's favorite recipes for a crowd, and I have included the recipe in a sidebar in chapter 6.

I had a few talks with Mrs. Biggs, and she showed me the portrait miniature medallions she was currently working on—she had a small studio/workshop that was neater and tidier than what you'd expect of most working artists' studios.

Mostly I spent the days prowling through oversized scrapbooks in which someone—perhaps Electra herself?—had pasted articles and clippings, in random order, often with no source. Today those scrapbooks are held by the Red River Valley Museum in Vernon, Texas, for safekeeping. After three generations in the headlines, the Waggoners have become a private family, and the museum has been given instructions that no one be allowed to view these caches of history, so they are unavailable to researchers. But they are safe. It may be that after years of litigation among various branches of the family, the Waggoners have learned to value privacy.

After two days, she announced it was time for me to leave and packed me into a pick-up driven by one of the ranch cowboys. I suspect her attention had turned wholly to her dinner party, and it may be that she realized we had different goals for my stay with her. I took the bus from Vernon back to Fort Worth. Thereafter, for some time, whenever the ranch plane flew into Fort Worth's Meacham Field, it would bring me more scrapbooks, and I would exchange the ones I had. That probably continued for the better part of a year.

What I wrote from that experience was unsatisfactory to me and to Electra Biggs. She and I saw the world differently—I was interested in her artistic accomplishments, highlighted by *Into the Sunset*, the life-sized statue of Will Rogers on his horse, Soapsuds, commissioned by Fort Worth newspaper tycoon Amon Carter, and placed in front of the Will Rogers Coliseum. Instead of her art, she was most interested in all the men who had whirled around her all her life and probably assumed that was the story I'd tell. I wrote up a bland fifty pages or so and gave them to her. This was long before computers, so I have no digital record and, to my great regret, no copy. Nor do I have any idea what happened to it. I am left with a lot of history and anecdotes jumbling around in my mind. I suspect much of my material was incorporated into the two laudatory books the late Roze McCoy Porter did about Thistle Hill, the Fort Worth Waggoner mansion, and Electra II, as she was often known. These were sanctioned works, flattering in nature, and I suspect Electra gave Porter my work, with changes and corrections she deemed necessary.

In 1986, the *Fort Worth Star-Telegram* commissioned me to write a serial novel about Texas history in celebration of Texas Sesquicentennial. Called *So Far from Paradise,* the family saga was loosely based on the first two generations of the Waggoner family, although at the time I discouraged efforts to identify the fictional family with any real people.

Recently, I pulled that novel out of my archive in the Southwest Writers Collection, reread it, and decided the full story of the Waggoners, the family and the ranch, needed to be told again. It is a remarkable story of the building of the largest ranch in the nation that was under one fence and of the family that built it and ultimately divided it. The Waggoner story has been told in newspapers, magazines, and in at least the two books mentioned above. This is my attempt to do it justice.

In many ways, ranching is a man's story. Dan Waggoner, born in Tennessee, established the ranch in the 1870s, registered it as Dan Waggoner and Son, near Vernon, Texas, with 230 head of cattle and a few horses. He gradually acquired land in several counties, and his son, W. T. (Tom), determined to have the most land of any Texas ranch and the best cattle and horses. W. T. continued to buy land, and in 1902 he found oil—or oil found him—when he drilled for nonexistent water. By the twenty-first century, the empire stretched over 520,000-plus acres or 800 square miles, covered six counties, and sat on a large oil field in the Red River Valley of North Texas. It was so large, with more than two thousand miles of road inside the fence, that Electra II once got lost. A cowboy riding by assured her she was still on her own land. Four generations of Waggoners lived on the land. Some cowboys and their families lived their whole lives on the ranch.

As I reread the history in various sources, snippets from what I learned years ago came back to me, memories for which I was hard put to find verification, and I realized what a fascinating story it is.

The ranch founder, Dan Waggoner, died in 1902, and his son, W. T., by then a Fort Worth city-dweller, in 1934. Although W. T. had two sons, it was the women of the family, a daughter and granddaughter, who kept the Waggoner name alive in the public eye. No doubt they got their strength from W. T.'s wife, Ella, born in 1859 in a prairie cabin when the Comanche and Kiowa were a constant presence and threat. In her lifetime, Ella went from that background to the twentieth century, where she had a skyscraper named after her, lived in glorious mansions, and administered the legendary ranch.

Ella's daughter and granddaughter, Electra I and Electra II, were more flamboyant than she, living life large. The first Electra was an international socialite, throwing lavish parties and literally dancing until dawn in Fort Worth and Dallas during the 1920s. The second Electra, the one I knew briefly, was also an international celebrity, having spent her twenties in New York in the 1930s hobnobbing with the likes of the Rockefellers, Chryslers, and others of wealth and social prominence. So great was her popularity that her second husband's brother-in-law, president of General Motors' Buick Division, named the Buick Electra after her. Rumor has it that the Lockheed Electra was also named after Mrs. Biggs (although there is less direct evidence to substantiate this claim). The plane may well be named after the Greek goddess Electra; the "shining bright and radiant" description surely fits the woman and the plane both, but it may be coincidence. Amelia Earhart was flying a modified version of that plane when she disappeared in 1937.

In contrast to Electra I, her storied aunt, Electra II spent much of her adult life on the ranch, though she was always ready to entertain and to travel. And she stayed married to one man. Her life of privilege was a far cry from that of her grandmother Ella and probably from what her grandfather envisioned for her. Still, she apparently shared the family fondness for disagreement and litigation and spent the last years of her life involved in contentious lawsuits over the future of the legendary ranch.

Today, the Waggoner Three D Ranch is owned by tycoon and sports mogul Stan Kroenke, the owner of the Los Angeles Rams, the husband of Walton heiress Ann Walton Kroenke, and with slightly over a million acres in his name. Kroenke also owns hockey, soccer, basketball, and lacrosse teams; ranches in Arizona, Montana, Wyoming, and British Columbia; three vineyards; and a luxury resort in California especially for wine merchants. In 2015, *The Land Report* ranked him as the ninth largest landowner. His 2016 purchase of the Waggoner ranch has made him owner of the largest ranch under one fence in the United States.

Kroenke has vowed to keep the Waggoner under one fence. No descendants of the Waggoner family live on the land for the first time in almost 150 years. It is the end of a saga. This is that story, and my attempt to place the family and the ranching empire in the context of place and time—North Texas in the last half of the nineteenth century up to the present.

PART I
The Waggoner Men

CHAPTER ONE

Daniel Waggoner

THE BUCKBOARD, LOADED WITH SUPPLIES, EMERGED FROM THE Cross Timbers, that strip of oaks, both live and post, that separates East Texas from the West, running the length of North Texas from southern Oklahoma south past where Dallas sits today. A tall, solid man, hat shoved over his eyes to avoid the Texas sun, held the reins of the horse. Beside him sat a young boy of perhaps two or three, fair of complexion like his father. A fifteen-year-old slave boy tended to the herd of 243 Longhorn cattle and 6 horses that trailed the wagon. It was 1854, and Dan Waggoner left his wife behind in a grave in Hopkins County in East Texas. Texas had been admitted to the United States eight years earlier, and no one yet knew the Civil War loomed ahead.

Dan Waggoner surveyed the land before him. To the west ahead of him lay open prairie, with grasses sometimes as tall as a man's waist and, if it was spring, wildflowers and plum thickets in full bloom that would challenge the palette of the best artist. Post oak and blackjack timber dotted the grand prairie, and an occasional creek cut through it, but the wide openness was what struck him. That and the endless sky above it.

"A man could see forever out here," he mused.

"What, Pa?" the boy next to him on the wagon seat asked.

"Cattle, son, cattle. We're going to have the biggest outfit ever."

"Yessir," the boy repeated emphatically. "The biggest outfit ever."

In the 1840s, when settlers from the East began pouring into Texas, the new state was forced to confront the violent conflicts between indigenous tribes who resisted the colonization of their ancestral lands, and White settlers immigrating into the region. The federal government had been unable to subdue the tribes. Toward the late 1840s, the government established a line of forts from Brownsville to Eagle Pass and the north to the confluence of the West Fork and the Clear Fork of the Trinity River, the spot where present-day Fort Worth is located. In the summer of 1849, Major Ripley Arnold established a fort at the site and named it Camp Worth, in honor of the recently deceased General William Jenkins Worth. Later that year, the government officially named the military encampment Fort Worth.

But the frontier was never static, always moving west, and even before some of the forts were completely occupied, the frontier had passed them by. A new line of forts was established some two hundred miles to the west of the first line. By the summer of 1859, the army evacuated the post at Fort Worth, leaving the buildings to the handful of settlers who were in the area.

When Dan Waggoner rode into the area, the forts had moved, and Fort Worth, the nearest to him, was a struggling frontier community. The Comanche and Kiowa continued their destructive raids in the territory left behind by the advancing forts, and a man took his life into his own hands if he settled on the plains of North Texas. If he brought his family, he risked their lives, too, for the tribes often waited until a man was away from home, chasing cattle or whatever, to attack the frontier cabins where women and children were unprotected.

Native Americans in North Texas

Ethnologists estimate that there were once hundreds of Native American bands in the region we now call Texas. Their history is cloudy at best, because the social structure ranged from large, organized bands to small family groups. The English, French, and Spanish each heard names and words differently, resulting in several names for any one group. Native people received guns from the French and English; from the Spanish, they adopted horses, which became all-important to their culture, dramatically changing their lives and allowing the nomadic bands greater mobility and increasing their warlike skills.

More powerful tribes displaced weaker ones and then, in turn, were replaced themselves. Thus, the Comanche, who were superb horsemen, literally rode onto the southern plains to force the fierce Apache to southern Texas and New Mexico. It was primarily the Comanche and their sometime-allies, the Kiowa, who clashed with cattle raisers in North Texas during the late nineteenth century. Neither the Comanche nor the Kiowa were one big tribe but were small autonomous bands, each responsible only for itself. A man could easily move from tribe to tribe if it suited him. What was difficult for settlers to understand was that a treaty with one band was not honored by all branches of the tribe.

The U.S. idea of Native American removal was first discussed as early as the 1820s and was policy by the 1830s as settlements moved into the traditional lands of Native Americans, pushing them ever westward. During the Texas War for Independence, Texans constantly feared that the Mexicans would recruit tribes to fight against them, while the natives watched and waited to see which side would win. Sam Houston favored a policy of fairness and friendship in dealing with the tribes, but his policies were overridden by Mirabeau B. Lamar, second president of the republic. Labeling the Native Americans "barbarians," Lamar refused to recognize native land rights and believed it was impossible for settlers and indigenous people to live in harmony.

The 1840 Council House fight in San Antonio decisively elevated tensions between the two populations. Comanche leaders were called to the Council House, a traditional meeting place, to negotiate a land treaty and return several hostages. Government leaders did not believe that the one captive the Comanche offered was the only one and demanded return of others. What they missed was that the lone girl may have been the only captive of this band, and they had no power over the captives held by other bands. Comanche leaders were held hostage, and when they rebelled, twelve were killed. The tribal members waiting outside went on a rampage, and when it was over, thirty-five Comanche and seven white men were dead, about thirty Comanche women and children were captured and held prisoner, and horses and hides were stolen.

This affront to the tribe triggered the massive raids on Linville and Victoria in August of 1840. A large band of Native Americans swept down on the two towns, killing citizens and enslaving people, taking many captives, and then plundering and burning the coastal town of Linville. They escaped with some three thousand horses. The Native Americans were subsequently defeated by a large army of volunteers at the Battle of Plum Creek (near present-day Lockhart).

After 1846, statehood brought more and more settlers to Texas, along with smallpox and cholera, which virtually wiped out some Native American bands. Tribes were also negatively impacted by their own hunting practices. Buffalo (American bison), which were a main food source for indigenous people, were dying out due to the overhunting of breeding-age females and the use of sharpshooters who were brought in specifically to decimate the great herds of the southern plains. The Comanche used every part of the bison that they did not eat, from tendons to bones, and without buffalo to hunt, they could not sustain their traditional way of life.

Tribes stole cattle that they could trade with Comancheros, the men who ventured into the Native American lands to buy cattle for trade in New Orleans markets. But by the 1870s, the Comancheros were gone and the bison scarce. The army began to attack in winter, destroying teepees and food supplies, a tactic heretofore avoided. Colonel Ranald S. McKenzie's attacks in which he destroyed the Native American horse herds were devastating. The Comanche world was shrinking.

Born in Tennessee in 1828, Dan Waggoner moved to East Texas, a part of the Mexican province of Coahuila y Tejas, as a boy with his family. They settled first in Hopkins County in the northeast corner of the territory, where his father was a farmer and traded in cattle, horses, and slaves.

Daniel Dale Waggoner

The Waggoner family was among many who came to Texas from the upper South—Tennessee, Kentucky, Missouri, and Arkansas. So many families from Tennessee followed the westward urge that some called the southern state the Grandfather of Texas. People loaded wagons with household goods and children and often a chicken coop or two, hitched a cow to the wagon, and drove a sow. They packed the necessities—sugar, salt, pepper, coffee, pork, flour, and yeast (if they had it and could keep it alive). Prepared for their adventurous journey, they boarded up their empty cabins, left signs that read "GTT"—Gone to Texas—and headed west.

They found country where the climate was mild and wood for cabins plentiful. Game was also abundant, and pigs, left to forage, grew fat. These settlers, new to the territory, lived on pork, not beef. And native corn. They brought with them the habits of a lifetime. Pretty much, they kept to themselves, proud of their independence and suspicious of strangers. It was a subsistence existence, and they uniformly expected poverty to just disappear one day. They set down no firm roots and willingly moved on to the next spot where they thought prosperity might beckon.

Dan Waggoner wanted more. He had married young to Nancy Moore, who died shortly after the birth of their son, W. T. (Tom). Like many men, Dan felt the westward pull. As the Comanche and Kiowa were pushed west, settlers followed, moving into what they thought was safe territory. Once out from the sheltering woods, they saw the difficulty of arable farming the open land and the allure of raising cattle. If he didn't have the cash to buy land, a man could prove up a land grant from the government, which used the grants to populate and improve empty land—three hundred acres. All he had to do was build a home on the land and live in it for three years. Many men—and a few hardy women—did this. Cattle could also be bought for not much, and sometimes a man could simply round up the unbranded cattle that roamed the plains and build a herd through hard work, but no cost.

Dan Waggoner's father, Solomon, died in 1849, and shortly thereafter Daniel purchased a small herd of Longhorn cattle and moved his remaining family—mother, brothers, sisters, and young son W. T. (Tom)—to a small farm on Catlett Creek in Cooke County (now Wise County). Although Dan once claimed that his father owned a slave woman named Aunt Nancy, estimating her age as 110, there is only a record of one slave boy accompanying the family west.

Dan Waggoner and his contemporaries were by no means pioneers in the Texas cattle industry. Ranching had been known in the Mexican territory as early as the seventeenth century. The word *ranch* derives from the Spanish *rancho* or headquarters of a *ranchero*, literally a place doing business raising livestock. Exploring Spaniards brought cattle to the land that were a mix of two or three European breeds. These cattle were tended by missionaries, soldiers, and civilians, but there were no fenced enclosures, and the cattle mostly ran wild for the better part of two centuries, hiding deep in the thickets and brambles of what today is South Texas.

In the early nineteenth century some settlers caught the feral cattle and bred them with cattle they had brought from the East. The result was the Longhorn as we know it today, a rangy cow, tall, skinny, and hardy, with horns extending to one hundred inches—the known record is 129. Longhorns come in many colors from bluish black to red and tan, some clear coated and others speckled. Their advantage was that they could survive on poor vegetation; the disadvantage, they were lean and stringy in an era when fat cattle were increasingly valued.

Texas's 1846 statehood did little to affect cattle raising, but the Civil War changed everything. Prior to the Civil War, cattle markets were few. Some ranchers drove cattle east, often to New

Orleans. Some cattle were shipped to coastal ports and taken to New Orleans and beyond by boat. These cattle generally came from the southern part of the state, but prior to the war ranching activity was shifting to North Texas.

Daniel Waggoner was on the leading edge of this shift of cattle to North Texas when he drove his small herd west and first settled on Catlett Creek. He set up camp near present-day Decatur, which was then just a trading post. Waggoner may have been ahead of the crowd, but settlers came to the area in a steady stream in the 1850s. In 1856, Wise County was organized. Waggoner continued to acquire cattle.

In 1855 he apparently partnered with a man named Brogden to establish ranchlands in what is today Parker County. Not having his "D" branding iron with him, Waggoner used a mule shoe to brand the cattle. The ranch became known as Muleshoe. Waggoner left Brogden in charge of the ranch and went off to acquire more cattle. After Brogden's untimely death, Waggoner could not purchase the land from the local school league, although there is no indication why the school league had property rights to the land. Waggoner was forced to round up his cattle and move them out.

Like the frontier, Waggoner moved ever west. In 1856, he purchased fifteen thousand acres eighteen miles west of Decatur, at a place known as Cactus Hill, and put an additional two hundred head of cattle on the land. His family remained near the now-growing community of Decatur, and he periodically broke from his travels acquiring land and cattle to visit them. In 1859, thirty-two-year-old Dan, a father and widower, married Cicily Halsell, the sixteen-year-old daughter of Elizabeth and Electious Halsell, who lived in Decatur. Electious operated a tavern, the first building to go up after the trading post, and Cicily helped her mother with the cooking and cleaning. On his visits to Decatur, Dan began to court Cicily. Waggoner took his bride and son, both in their late teens, to his log cabin at Cactus

Hill, eighteen miles west of Decatur. They lived there until after the Civil War. At this point in Waggoner's story, the rest of his family drops out of the picture.

When war came with the fall of Fort Sumter in 1861, men throughout the state left to fight. Congress passed a conscription law—the first draft law in the United States—requiring men between the ages of twenty and forty-five to register for military service. Under the law, a man could either pay a conscription fee or find someone to serve in his place. A good number of Texans did this, feeling obligated to stay to protect the frontier and their families. Dan Waggoner probably bought himself out of the service, though there is no record of that.

Civil War Violence in North Texas

Electious Halsell was lucky to escape hanging the day he was almost lynched in his tavern. Violence against suspected Union sympathizers in North Texas began as early as 1860, when several slaves and a northern Methodist minister were lynched in North Texas. Cooke County, north of Denton, voted against secession—fewer than 10 percent of households in the county owned slaves—and this aroused the anger and suspicion of landed slaveholders.

The Conscription Act of 1862 increased the divisive anger because it exempted large slaveholders from conscription. Some men sent a petition protesting this to the Confederate government in Richmond, and the Confederate military commander, Brigadier General William Hudson, exiled the Unionist leader, hoping to diffuse the resistance. Instead, the remaining men formed the Union League, which had several small groups in the region. The various groups within the league had differing goals, but they were unified in wanting to avoid the draft and to band together to fight raids by the Comanche and Kiowa. When rumors flew that some 1,700 members of the league were planning an insurrection, Hudson sent armed troops to the area with instructions to arrest all men who did not report for duty.

On October 1, 1862, 150 men were arrested and brought before a "citizens court" in Gainesville, county seat of Cooke County. Seven of the twelve jurors were slaveholders; none of the arrested men owned slaves. Seven influential Unionists were convicted of treason, and before the jury could act, a mob lynched fourteen more. When an unknown assailant killed two slaveholders, the men scheduled for release were instead retried, and nineteen more men were hanged. All in all, that month forty-two men were hanged in Cooke County and two shot when they tried to escape.

Several men were also killed in neighboring counties, all accused of insurrection and treason, though it is believed few of them held abolitionist beliefs. That figure probably includes the five or six men who were hung outside Decatur. That hanging, referred to by Harry Halsell in his memoir, was also supervised by a citizens' court under the direction of a Confederate officer. The Confederate government in Richmond, in cooperation with Texas authorities, disbanded citizens' courts, but the action came too late for many men. After the war, only one man was convicted in the hangings. Several Unionists, who had fled the area with victims' families, returned to reestablish their lives, and today many descendants of the hanging victims live in Gainesville.

Today the town is still divided in reaction to what is known as the Great Hanging. Some citizens want to downplay it and capitalize on the fact that in 2012 Rand McNally named Gainesville "the Most Patriotic Small Town in Texas." There is a Confederate memorial near the downtown. But in 2014, a new memorial was dedicated. A large gray slab tells the story of the Great Hanging, and a matching slab lists the forty-two men who died. Descendants of those men feel the memorial brings recognition that they have sought for a long time.

Native American raids had continued to be a problem even with troops to the west, because the federal army was some distance away and slow moving. With the Civil War, federal troops were withdrawn, leaving settlers even more vulnerable to attacks by raiding Comanche, Kiowa, Caddo, and other tribes who had been removed to the reservation north of the Red

River. Although several tribes raided, the Comanche were the most dreaded. They often came after horses and cattle rather than scalps, but, when met with resistance or counterattack, they could be brutal. And they harbored a fierce resentment toward settlers who had displaced them from their ancestral lands.

Going off to war, men left behind families, who sheltered in towns for protection against the Native Americans, and cattle that were left to roam the prairie and forage as they could. Many of these men would return to deserted homesteads, their families moved or buried in the ground, cattle scattered. They were often bitter and disillusioned, and they frequently gathered in Electious Halsell's tavern to share grievances. Some resented those who had stayed behind to raise cattle, although men such as Waggoner supplied meat to the Confederate Army. In 1863, Union forces closed the Mississippi River. Then Texans had no place to take their cattle, and the number of animals on the plains rapidly multiplied. Thousands of unbranded cattle or "mavericks" roamed the plains of north Texas.

Maverick

History has forever linked the name of Samuel A. Maverick to unbranded cattle roaming the range or independent individuals who go their own way, away from the crowd. That's unfortunate, because Maverick made solid contributions to Texas independence.

A lawyer, born and raised in South Carolina and educated at Yale, Maverick arrived in San Antonio in 1835 during the Texas Revolution, just before the siege of Bexar, and was put under house arrest by Mexican General Martín Perfecto de Cos. Maverick's diaries kept during this period provided valuable information. Once released, he hurried to meet with the Texas army and urge immediate attack on San Antonio.

Later he was elected a delegate from the Alamo garrison to the Texas Independence Convention and was in Washington-on-the-Brazos when the Alamo fell. While at the convention, he became ill, probably a recurrence of malaria, and after the group dispersed, he returned to South Carolina to recover his health and take care of business matters.

Maverick returned to Texas in 1838, bringing his wife, Mary Ann Maverick, their son, Samuel A. Maverick Jr., and a small number of slaves. Maverick practiced law in San Antonio and was briefly taken prisoner by Mexican general Adrián Woll. Upon his release, he served in the seventh and eighth congresses of the Republic of Texas. In 1844, he moved his family to Matagorda Bay, where they lived until 1847, when they returned permanently to San Antonio.

He left behind in Matagorda a herd of cattle with slaves to watch over them. But the unbranded cattle were allowed to wander, and that's when the Maverick name became associated with stray cattle. Legend sometimes attributes the wandering cattle to laziness on Maverick's part, but that was not true.

Maverick acquired a great deal of land mostly through buying headright and bounty certificates, and in the 1850s and 1860s he was one of the two largest landholders in West Texas. After statehood, Maverick served a couple of terms in the state legislature. He fought secession, but when it seemed inevitable, he gave his support to the Confederacy and worked for the removal of federal troops from Texas. He twice served as mayor of San Antonio and was elected a chief justice of Bexar County. He died in 1872, survived by his wife and five of his ten children.

Of equal interest is Maverick's wife, Mary Ann, whose diaries chronicled pioneer life, particularly her eyewitness account of the Council House Fight in San Antonio. Mary Ann Maverick bore ten children in twenty-one years and saw four of them die of disease under the age of eight. She sent four sons to fight for the Confederacy. After her husband's death, she was determined to see that the trials of pioneer life were not forgotten and worked with the Daughters of the Republic of Texas and the San Antonio Historical Society and served several years as the president of the Alamo Historical Society, working for its preservation long before the early twentieth-century restoration of the mission. She published a limited number of copies of her memoir; it was later reprinted and given wider distribution. Today, the work provides an invaluable picture of life in south Texas in the mid- and late nineteenth century.

Dan Waggoner continued to buy land and cattle, traveling the country in ever-widening circles, leading a packhorse loaded with gold. By the 1860s, he owned fifteen thousand acres of land, a good-sized piece when most men were having trouble holding onto their land and cattle because of the Native American raids. He branded his ever-growing cattle herd with the letter *D* on the right hip. Later that brand would be changed to the backward three *D*s. Stories surround the use of that backward *D*. Some say the blacksmith who forged the branding iron had it upside down when he held the paper on which Waggoner had written his brand. But the probable explanation was that it was done deliberately, because the backward three *D*s was a difficult brand for rustlers to change with a running iron.

To fight the danger from Indian raids, men formed militia bands to chase raiders, mostly Comanche and Kiowa. Waggoner was part of such a band and was often away from home. More than once, Cicily took young W. T. and a rifle to the cornfield at night, where they hid among the rows. By the light of the moon, they'd watch shadows slinking around their cabin. The Comanche were most likely to raid on nights with a full moon, and settlers came to call that a "Comanche moon."

On one such night, while the pair was hiding among the cornfields, a dog gave one startled yelp. Tom turned to Cicily, his eyes wide. She merely pressed her finger to her lips and clutched her rifle tighter. Finally, the youngster fell asleep, and Cicily covered him with a blanket. In the morning, they would discover a mare and the dog dead, their bodies pierced with arrows.

For protection, Dan Waggoner moved his family closer to Decatur, but he continued to ride with the militia throughout the war and after. The threat of attack did not disappear with the end of the war—if anything, it became more severe because the tribes felt they were being crowded off their land. Once Waggoner was in a cabin with several men when they were attacked by sixteen Comanche braves. Although they were able to chase off their attackers, two men were hit with arrows. Waggoner was the one who removed the arrows and dressed the wounds. He was rapidly becoming a legend in his part of North Texas.

Dan Waggoner developed a close relationship with his young son, taking him along on short rides on the range, talking to him about ranching and livestock as though he were already the partner he would become, even letting him help with branding. Dan probably realized he was setting the stage for that "biggest outfit ever."

By the age of fourteen, young Tom was doing a man's work and was an excellent marksman. He rode herd with the other cowboys and later rode from a line camp out on the prairie away from the main headquarters with his uncle, George Halsell.

Several cattlemen tried to drive herds north to Sedalia, Missouri, for shipment to the stockyards at Chicago, but the route took them through eastern Kansas, and farmers there objected to the drives. They knew the passing cattle would destroy crops and damage property, and they feared that they carried cattle fever, variously known as Texas fever or tick fever. The farmers armed themselves and successfully blocked the drives.

In the late 1860s, the railroad reached Abilene, Kansas, in the central part of the state, and Joseph McCoy opened a cattle-shipping operation. The route from Texas to Abilene crossed western Kansas, out of reach of the contentious farmers. Known as the Chisholm Trail, after the Scottish-Cherokee fur trader who scouted it, the route was far from a precise road but rather cut a wide swath through Indian Territory. Later, other trails, such as Goodnight-Loving, would take the cattle even farther west.

In 1870 an unknown party offered to buy Dan Waggoner out of the land and cattle business. Dan listened instead to W. T.'s argument that he should turn the business over to him. Dan sent his first herd to Abilene, with seventeen-year-old W. T. in charge of the drive with seasoned cowboys riding herd for him and a chuck wagon to provide meals. Waggoner supposedly gave W. T. $12 for supplies, cautioning the youth to hold back and let other herds get ahead of him. His theory was that Tom would then pick up their strays and add them to his herd, thereby decreasing his expenses by giving him extra cattle to butcher to feed his cowboys.

W. T. Waggoner left no record of the actual drive, but cattle drive literature abounds. The best and most realistic account of the monotony and dangers is found in Andy Adams's *The Log of a Cowboy: A Narrative of the Old Trail Days* (1903). Although young cowboys like W. T. were always anxious and ready for excitement on the trail, the truth is that a trail drive could be boring. Cattle grazed as they moved north, so the pace was deadly slow, and a drive took not just weeks but months. They usually set out from Texas in the spring, when the land greened up enough for grazing, and often the cowboys didn't return home until late summer.

Food on this slow drive was monotonous, though records indicate that a cowboy chuck wagon gave birth to chili, that state dish of Texas. And some cooks, or cousies as they were called (from the Spanish *cocina* or kitchen), fixed that cowboy delicacy son-of-a-bitch stew, which used all part of a beef. And the coffee pot was always on for whenever a cowboy had a chance to slip back to the wagon.

At night, cowboys took turns sleeping and riding guard over the bedded cows. Many a cowboy sang soft tunes to soothe the animals, because the slightest thing could set them off. All it took was one agitated cow, and a stampede erupted. Lightning could spook them, or a blowing tumbleweed, or a horse bucking, or just a wild notion on the part of that one cow. Sometimes the Comanche would sneak up on a herd at night and wave blankets at them, inciting a stampede.

Cattle run blindly, and in a stampede, they trample everything in their way, including men and horses. Whole herds have been known to run off a cliff or into a river. At the least, when the exhausted cattle finally stopped, they were scattered all over North Texas or Indian Territory, and the cowboys lost days rounding them up.

Other dangers of the trail were also very real. If the Red River was high, cowboys had to swim the cattle across, and more than one cowboy—and some cattle—drowned in those muddy waters. The river carried brush and branches that would sweep a man away, and cattle often bogged down in the red mud and had to be pulled out with horses.

The Comanche frequently stopped the herds to demand a beef or two for allowing the drive to cross their land unmolested. Actual battles between cowboy and Native American were rare, despite the myth that has grown up around cattle drives.

W. T.'s drive made it to Abilene without serious difficulty, and the young man sold his cattle for $55,000, which he promptly put in a bank for safekeeping. Arriving the next day to meet his son and the other drovers, Dan Waggoner flew into a panic when he heard the money was in the bank.

"Most dangerous place in the world to put money," he fussed. "Tom, go buy a cheap cardboard suitcase."

Tom was taken aback, because he thought he'd done the careful thing. When he questioned his father (something he rarely did), Dan explained that banks go out of business without notice all the time, something especially true in that time and place.

The Waggoners went home carrying $55,000 in a cheap suitcase. It was the money they needed to expand their operations and build an empire. W. T. began buying cattle at $8 a head.

By 1870 Waggoner had named his business D. Waggoner and Son. He had added Hereford and Shorthorn or Durham cattle to his Longhorn. The Hereford, bred in England and introduced pre–Civil War in the eastern United States, gave a high yield of beef when grass fed and reached maturity more quickly than some other breeds. Herefords were called the "improvers," because they improved the weight and market value of herds. Shorthorn or Durham cattle, also originally from England, were originally used both for dairy and beef production but gradually split into two lines. Waggoner's Shorthorns were beef cattle, short-legged, stocky animals. Pictures of them at early stock shows in the late nineteenth century show how they contrast with today's taller, leaner cattle.

The years of the cattle drives were short. By 1886, the railroad reached western Kansas and then Wichita Falls in North Texas. The Waggoners made their last drive in 1886. By then, they had bought land clear north to the Red River, in the counties of Wilbarger, Foard, Wichita, Baylor, Archer, and Knox. As they bought and sold more herds, they used the profits for more land. Someone asked Dan if he wanted to buy all the land in North Texas, and he replied, "No, just what adjoins mine." W. T. would later express his philosophy about land this way: "They are making people every day, but they are not making land."

The Waggoners persuaded the Fort Worth and Denver Railroad to build a spur line of tracks to a spot where they could conveniently build loading pens for shipping cattle. The settlement that grew up around the pens was briefly called Waggoner, but when a post office was established, it was changed to Beaver, because it lay on Beaver Creek, which also ran through much of the Waggoner land. Today, the small city is known as Electra, having changed its name in 1902 to honor W. T.'s daughter, Electra.

Despite his focus on land and cattle, Waggoner did not forget Cicily. In the 1880s, he built a mansion in Decatur for her. The house is a two-story Victorian masonry structure with sixteen rooms, six and a half bathrooms, and a basement, and is situated on thirteen-and-a-half acres of rolling land. Still standing, it is known as El Castile. Exterior trim features like the original railing around the roof, cornice detailing, and porch construction emphasized the Victorian era in which the house was first built. The interior boasts sixteen-foot and eighteen-foot ceilings, elaborate carved moldings with a Texas Lone Star motif throughout, carved door moldings, stained glass transoms, frescoed ceilings, brass fixtures, and interior shutters on all windows. The latter may be a nod to the need for protection on the frontier, when log cabins had wooden shutters that could be closed against attack. In its day, the home was the epitome of luxury, and today it stands as a symbol of the heyday of the cattle barons.

There's a story about El Castile that illustrates W. T.'s modesty—and his frugality. It seems that the men of Decatur, W. T. included, liked to watch the train come in. One day the train brought in a drummer who mistook W. T. for a poor cowboy and offered him a quarter if he'd carry his bag. W. T. picked up the man's bag, and they began walking. The drummer saw El Castile in the distance and asked who lived in that grand house. Without further comment, W. T. said, "I do." Amazed, the drummer asked, "How can you afford that?" Waggoner replied, "I carry my own bag."

Burk Burnett

W. T. Waggoner was by nature a modest man, soft-spoken and given to avoiding the limelight. Some of his closest companions, however, were just the opposite. Perhaps his oldest friend was fellow cattleman Burk Burnett. Like W. T., Burnett had little if any formal schooling but learned the cattle business from his father. Burnett's first cattle drive was to Abilene in 1866. In 1876 he settled in the area of Wichita Falls, Texas, and later bought land north of Amarillo and in New Mexico and Oklahoma. Today two ranches bear his Four Sixes brand, both in West Texas, one near the town of Panhandle and the other near Guthrie. The ranching empire, once owned by the late Mrs. Anne Marion, Burnett's great-granddaughter, was sold to filmmaker Taylor Sheridan in the spring of 2021.

Like Waggoner, Burnett had a great admiration and a keen eye for horse flesh. The Four Sixes is noted today for its Thoroughbred stallions. The two horsemen had a friendly rivalry that began with informal races in North Texas and often involved wagering money, not just on horses. There's a story that Burnett challenged Waggoner, saying he bet the latter did not know the Lord's Prayer. Indignantly, Waggoner began to recite, "Now I lay me down to sleep." When he finished, Burnett said, "Damn! I didn't think you knew it," and he paid off.

Along with Waggoner, Burnett was influential in leasing the Big Pasture and negotiating with Quanah Parker. He also helped arrange the wolf hunt for President Theodore Roosevelt. By 1900, Burnett maintained a Fort Worth headquarters for his ranching, oil, and banking interests. He was a charter member and one-time treasurer of the Texas and Southwestern Cattle Raisers Association and former president of the Fort Worth Fat Stock Show.

Burnett's granddaughter, Anne Valiant Burnett Tandy, was briefly married to W. T.'s son, Guy. At the time of his death in 1922, Burnett was married to his second wife, Mary Couts Burnett. After some discord between the two over Burnett's close relationship to his granddaughter, Burnett had his wife declared mentally unfit and committed to an institution or confined to a private home in a town near Fort Worth (history gives both versions). Following his death, she was released and the insanity ruling reversed. Burnett had left everything to his granddaughter, but Mary Couts Burnett sued and was granted half the $6 million estate. Mrs. Burnett gave most of her inheritance to Texas Christian University, where it was primarily used to establish the Mary Couts Burnett Library. Rumor persists to this day that she made the gift because she knew how much her late husband hated higher education.

For the next thirty years D. Waggoner and Son continued to invest in land and cattle. In the mid-1880s, the father and son had acquired cattle so successfully that their extensive land holdings in North Texas were not enough. In order to get more grassland, they leased land in the Big Pasture in Oklahoma's Comanche/Kiowa-Indian Territory, a part of the Indian reservation near Frederick, Oklahoma. The government had set aside the land for grazing, but the Native Americans did not have enough livestock to take full advantage of it. *The Handbook of Texas* states that the Waggoners leased 650,000 acres, but C. L. Douglas claims that Waggoner and Burk Burnett together leased only 300,000 acres. *The Encyclopedia of Oklahoma History and Culture* indicates the Big Pasture consisted of 480,000 acres. Regardless of its size, the land provided needed room for Texas cattlemen, who were glad to pasture herds there. They paid rent of an annual fee of six-and-a-half cents an acre to the U.S. government, which in turn sent periodic lease payments to the various tribes.

Burnett, the Waggoners, and other ranchers may have leased the land from the government, but they understood the need to keep in Comanche Chief Quanah Parker's good graces. They presented him with a diamond stick pin and pearl-handled revolvers; they invited him to Fort Worth for meetings and to Washington, D.C., where he met President Theodore Roosevelt. And they built him a two-story house near the town of Cache, a home large enough to accommodate his seven wives and numerous children. The only permanent building between Fort Sill and the Texas border at the time, it boasted fourteen stars on its roof—symbols, he insisted, of his status as a chief. It was generally known as the Comanche White House.

The cattlemen's indulgences of the chief resulted in one tragedy. At the invitation of the Waggoners and others, Quanah and another chief, Yellow Bear, paid a visit to Fort Worth in 1887, probably to discuss the leasing arrangements. The cattlemen likely wined and dined their guests. History tells us the two chiefs retired for the night to their elegant room in the new El Paso Hotel. Upon retiring, they blew out the gas lamp, with comments about the bad smell.

Ranch hands on the W. T. Waggoner Ranch: Ira Cockrell, Earl Moon, and Tommie Reed, June 10, 1935.

Quanah awoke during the night and tried to drag himself and Yellow Bear to a window but apparently collapsed without reaching it. They were found after thirteen hours. Quanah recovered, but Yellow Bear died. Quanah accompanied his friend's body back to the reservation, where his story met with skepticism. The Comanche could not believe that a man could blow out a light, lie down to sleep—and die. According to Douglas, the cattlemen saved the day by bringing bottles of ammonia to the reservation. They waved them under the Native Americans' noses, proving that "bad air" was a real thing.

Cynthia Ann and Quanah Parker

Quanah Parker was the Comanche chief primarily responsible for working with the government to open the grasslands of the Oklahoma reservation—the Big Pasture—for Texas cattlemen. Born into the Nocona Comanche tribe, he was the son of the illustrious war chief Peta Nocona and the most famous White captive, Cynthia Ann Parker.

Cynthia Ann's family established Fort Parker on the Navasota River in Central Texas, near present Mexia. In 1836, when she was eleven or twelve, Comanche attacked the family compound, killing most of her extended family but taking five captives, Cynthia Ann among them. The other four were subsequently released, but Cynthia Ann remained with the Comanches, adapting to their ways and forgetting White customs. Peta Nocona took her as his wife, and she bore him two sons and a daughter, Topsannah. Efforts to ransom or rescue her failed, and she rejected pleas to return to her own people.

In 1860, Captain Lawrence Sullivan "Sul" Ross of the Texas Rangers attacked a small Comanche camp near the Pease River in North Texas. Rangers claimed that Peta Nocona was killed in the battle, but Quanah would later insist that it was his father's Mexican slave who died, and that Peta Nocona survived for a year, only to die of a wound he acquired from the battle.

When the Rangers rounded up the women and children, they noticed one woman who had blue eyes but otherwise looked thoroughly Comanche. Legend has it that when they singled her out, she muttered, "Me cinsee ann." She and her infant daughter were "rescued" and returned to her uncle, Colonel Isaac Parker. She accompanied him to Birdville, Texas (near Fort Worth), after being assured her sons would join her as soon as they were found. The Parker cabin to which she was returned can now be seen at Fort Worth's Log Cabin Village.

Contrary to her family's expectations, Cynthia Ann did not immediately adjust to White ways, and they found her Indian ways troublesome. She, meanwhile, became despondent, fearing that Nocona was dead, and she would never see her Comanche family again. She was passed to different family members and made several unsuccessful attempts to escape. Topsannah died, and Cynthia Ann followed her shortly after. Some said she died of a broken heart. She and her daughter were buried in Texas, but many years later Quanah had their bodies moved to the cemetery near his home in Cache, Oklahoma.

Quanah, still in his teens when he was orphaned, took refuge with the Quahada tribe and became a fierce fighter against White settlement. Like Tom Waggoner, he had a dream: to avenge his mother's recapture, steal the most horses, and become the greatest Comanche warrior. For several years, he ruled the plains, leading raids and disappearing into the prairie, where military forces could not find him. He was one of the leaders of the multi-tribe 1873 assault on buffalo hunters holed up in an abandoned outpost known as Adobe Walls. The attack was a disaster for the natives, with several killed and more, including Quanah, wounded.

By 1874, Quanah recognized the inevitable and led his people into the reservation at Fort Sill. Thereafter he was instrumental in encouraging his people to "walk the white man's road." He remained a contradiction, wearing white man's fancy clothes off the reservation and Comanche clothes on it. Urging his people to follow Christianity, he was devoted to the Native American religion or Peyote Church. He was a polygamist who refused pleas to give up his several wives—hence the large house near Cache. He supported education, and with the help of men like W. T. Waggoner and Burk Burnett, Quanah developed ranching among his people, making himself wealthy in the process. He encouraged his followers to build houses in the White man's style and to plant crops, since they had been forced to give up their nomadic ways.

Quanah Parker, who kept one foot each in the White and Comanche worlds, died in 1911 and was buried next to his mother. When circumstances forced the removal of the cemetery and the reburial of the bodies, he was given full military honors.

Times were tough for cattlemen in the Big Pasture. Tribal members occasionally took a few cattle, but rustlers were a far bigger problem. To deal with them, the Waggoners hired a slight young man named Jimmie Roberts as a peeler. Roberts rode up to headquarters one day armed with a rifle, a shotgun, and two six-shooters. It was his job to check passing herds and cut out or peel off any steers that carried the Three D brand. After Roberts shot "one or two" rustlers out of the saddle, thieves gained great respect for the Three D brand, and their cattle were left alone. Jimmie Roberts became one of the most valuable ranch hands.

In the 1880s, the Waggoners sold some forty thousand head of cattle per year, and W. T. continued to expand his father's dream, buying land sometimes as low as a dollar an acre. Some say Roberts also helped "persuade" small farmers to sell their acreage to the Waggoners. Others claim little persuasion was needed. A drought near the end of the nineteenth century killed any chance of raising farm crops on the land. Without water, farmers were glad to sell at any price. Many of them, mostly Czech and German immigrants, clustered near the town of Lockett, just beyond the northern edge of the ranch where underground water was and is still plentiful. Going into the twenty-first century, Lockett claimed a population of two hundred.

Dan Waggoner died in 1902 in Colorado Springs, where he had gone in hope of a cure for chronic kidney disease. He was seventy-four years old and survived only by his present wife, Cicily, and one son, W. T. Dan and Cicily had moved from El Castile to a home at 1418 El Paso Street in Fort Worth. They set an example that would later see many Waggoners move from the ranch to the city of Fort Worth. The *Fort Worth Star-Telegram* hailed his place in history, saying, "Probably no man in Northern Texas had more to do with the history of that part of the state." A great many people attended the funeral, which was held in the Waggoner residence, and the procession to the cemetery was said to be the largest yet seen in the city, according to Roze Porter in her study, *Thistle Hill: The Cattle Baron's Legacy*. Most sources indicate, however, that Dan Waggoner was buried in the family mausoleum in Decatur.

W. T. Waggoner was devastated by the death of his father, whom he had long worshipped. They had been D. Waggoner and Son for fifty-two years. Many years later, the Waggoner bank in Decatur sustained a loss that made necessary the issuance of new certificates of stock. Tom went into his own pocket to cover the assessment on stockholders, because he wanted to retain the original stock with his father's signature.

With his father's death, W. T. Waggoner took over the huge cattle enterprise. By that time, D. Waggoner and Son owned 80,000 head of cattle and 525,000 acres. In addition, W. T. had leases on another 100,000 acres in the Indian Territory. He also owned five banks, three cottonseed oil mills, and a coal company. He had realized his father's dream of the biggest and best cattle outfit in the country. Horses would come next.

Chapter Two

W. T. Waggoner

In 1877, twenty-seven-year-old W. T. Waggoner married eighteen-year-old Ella Halsell, the younger sister of his stepmother, Cicily Halsell Waggoner. The wedding was apparently a low-key affair, though one text refers to an exciting wagon ride over the prairie to Denton. Tom had hitched up his two favorite horses and ridden to Decatur to pick up his bride. They were married by a Justice of the Peace in Denton, probably because they had to go there to get a marriage license. The bride wore a brown bespoke dress of her own making and was attended by twelve male friends of the groom. Left unknown is her family's reaction to what seems to be a planned elopement. There is no record of their attendance at the ceremony.

After a honeymoon in Sherman, Texas, the couple settled down to raising cattle—and babies. Five children were born to the union, but only three survived to reach adulthood. First-born Daniel arrived in 1879 and died in 1882; Electra, the only daughter, was born in 1882, and Guy Leslie, in 1883. Willie Tom, born in 1886, did not survive childhood. The youngest Waggoner child was E. Paul, born in 1888.

Perhaps because of his five children, W. T. Waggoner became commonly known to adults and children alike as Pappy Waggoner. At some point, W. T. moved his growing family into the mansion in Decatur, possibly after his father and stepmother moved to Fort Worth in 1891. In those years, Dan and Cicily were frequent Sunday dinner guests at El Castile, a habit that no doubt allowed Dan and W. T. to exchange business ideas and news.

With his family settled, W. T. continued his father's business of building an empire, always striving to meet his own goal of being the biggest and best cattle rancher.

By the turn of the twentieth century, settlers were clamoring for land in Oklahoma, and the federal government was making noises about forcing Texas cattlemen to take their cattle back to Texas and vacate the leased grasslands. Ranchers were devastated by this prospect: they had invested time and money in fencing their Oklahoma pastures with barbed wire, and if they had to drive cattle back across the Red River, they would surely lose animals and perhaps even men. Chief Quanah Parker did not like the idea either, for his people had grown accustomed to the income from the ranchers' lease money. Satisfaction to his own ego was probably also a factor in Quanah's desire to keep the cattle in the Big Pasture. The Texas ranchers' coalition, a rather shaky agreement among men who didn't always get along with each other, had sent Quanah to D.C. often enough that the Comanche and President Teddy Roosevelt had struck up a friendship. When the threats became strong, Burk Burnett traveled to see Roosevelt and try to persuade him to keep the pastureland open to Texas ranchers. Burnett was able to secure a grace period, with the president promising to delay the order to open the land for at least two years. He promised he would personally visit the Indian Territory to check on things, a cover for going on a wolf hunt. President Roosevelt's 1905 wolf hunt in the Big Pasture became legend in the retelling of Waggoner history.

According to the *Fort Worth Star-Telegram*, Roosevelt arrived in Fort Worth by train on April 8, 1905, at 9:45 a.m. and departed at 11:03 a.m. An estimated crowd of thirty thousand stood in line to honor the first U.S. president to visit the city. During his brief visit, he rode in an open carriage so that he could greet the crowd and planted a tree in front of the Carnegie library. His Fort Worth visit was part of a swing through Texas; he had earlier visited several cities and spoken in front of the Alamo and the state capitol in Austin. From Fort Worth, his party was headed by train to Vernon, where, with his hosts W. T. Waggoner and Burk Burnett, he boarded a special train to Frederick, Oklahoma. Knowing Roosevelt's history with the American West and his love of outdoors and sports, one might suspect the entire trip was planned with the Oklahoma jaunt in mind.

Roosevelt was lured to the Big Pasture by the reputation of wolf hunter Jack Abernathy, who would lead the hunt. Abernathy, a rough and rowdy Texas cowboy, had settled his family to homestead in Oklahoma. Once when attacked by a wolf, he saved himself by reaching into the animal's mouth, grasping its lower jaw and bending it down, rendering it unable to bite him. After that attack, Abernathy routinely caught wolves by hand, injuring neither himself nor the wolf. He made a living selling wolves to zoos and entertainment companies. The bounty for a live wolf was $50. Abernathy also caught coyotes, but his sources did not pay nearly as much for them as for the wolves.

Several other Texas ranchers were in the hunting party, including W. T.'s son, Guy. Each brought their best cow ponies for the president to ride and their best greyhounds to chase wolves. In a way, the ranchers were competing with each other for Roosevelt's favor. Several other cattlemen and dignitaries were also invited. Quanah Parker came to the hunt, bringing three wives and two children. A large camp was set up some twenty miles from Frederick near the Red River, where there was plenty of fresh water, green grass—and wolves.

The hunt lasted for six days, and during that time Abernathy is said to have caught fifteen wolves. The president lived up to his reputation as an outdoorsman, racing over the prairie on the fastest horses he could borrow. At one point, he and Abernathy outraced all the other riders chasing a wolf, certainly an exciting and triumphant moment for an outdoorsman such as Roosevelt. He was riding one of W. T.'s strongest horses that day.

The hunt ended with a wild horse race into Frederick, where the president again addressed a crowd. When he arrived in Frederick, he had told onlookers that he liked his job and his citizens, but he did not want them on a wolf hunt with him. He asked for and got privacy, and when he left Frederick at the end of the hunt, he thanked the citizens. He then boarded a train for Colorado, where he was going bear hunting. A year later in 1906, the territory was opened to settlers, and Burk Burnett and W. T. were among those who drove their cattle back to Texas. The wolf hunt had been great and wild fun, but it had not had the long-term effect the ranchers wanted. In 1907, Oklahoma became a state.

That year the town of Electra held a grand opening, to which, of course, the Waggoners were invited. W. T. had sold the land on which Electra sat to a town site developer from Fort Worth, retaining a large livery stable and its land for himself. He also sold 91,000 acres between Electra and the Red River to a developer, who divided it into 160-acre farming tracts. That area was known as Waggoner's Colony. The subsequent opening of Electra as a town thus attracted not only would-be residents of Electra but also land seekers. The event had the atmosphere of a carnival, complete with a revival tent, a band, and a livestock show.

Meanwhile, Ella and W. T. had moved to Fort Worth in 1906, settling in a house at 530 Hill Street (later Summit Avenue). Their children were growing or grown, even young Electra. But none of the three surviving children showed much interest in ranching, let alone in carrying on their father's ambition to be the biggest and best rancher. Nor did they seem to identify at all with their mother's hardscrabble childhood in a log cabin.

W. T. did an unprecedented thing at Christmas 1909: he gifted his children with land and cattle valued at $6,000,000, making them independently wealthy. By then, Electra had married Albert Buckman Wharton, a Philadelphia socialite, and produced two sons. Guy Waggoner had married and divorced and already married again to the second of his eight wives, with a son by each wife, giving W. T. four grandsons. E. Paul would marry Helen Buck of Sherman in the spring of 1910. His was the only marriage that lasted a lifetime, surviving some rough patches because of E. Paul's alleged philandering.

W. T. divided the ranch into four parcels, keeping the east side (and presumably largest parcel) for himself. He called it White Face, probably an acknowledgment of the white-faced Hereford cattle he was breeding. The other three parcels were Zacaweista (variously spelled Sachuiesta), Four Corners, and Santa Rosa, each tract containing between 85,000 and 95,000 acres (sources vary), stocked with thousands of cattle and hundreds of horses. The Waggoner heirs drew to see who got which parcel. Electra wanted Zacaweista (the name is indigenous for "good grass"), and W. T. wanted her to have it because it was closer to his land. But it went to E. Paul, who didn't really care and obligingly traded with his sister. Some sources also claim that W. T. had them draw again. W. T. was not simply being altruistic with these Christmas gifts. He no doubt hoped his offspring would settle down and develop a sense of responsibility. They didn't. But the munificent gifts put the three Waggoner offspring squarely in the public spotlight, with everyone from newspapers to local gossips reporting on their every move. At least at first, it must have seemed that W. T. could make money as fast as his children could spend it.

In his *Texas Monthly* article, "Showdown at the Waggoner Ranch," Gary Cartwright suggested that when he "rigged the game," W. T. laid the seeds of dissension that would eventually lead to the endless lawsuits in the late twentieth and early twenty-first centuries, as the branches of the family sued each other. At any rate, in 1923 after their grown children had squandered unbelievable amounts of money on everything from countless divorces to all-night poker parties, W. T. and Ella apparently decided the gifts were a bad idea. They probably worried that the record number of marriages and divorces among their children would lead to settlement issues that might diminish the estate. Electra was then married to her second husband; Guy, to his third wife; and Electra's son, Tom, had recently married.

The senior Waggoners took the land back and consolidated it all into what became the Waggoner Estate. W. T. set up a trust fund for Electra, Guy, and E. Paul and put control of the ranch under an arrangement sometimes called a Massachusetts business trust or an unincorporated business organization. Under the terms of this document, there would be a board of directors, elected by the three Waggoner heirs. Each of the children owned one-third of the one hundred thousand shares of the estate, but the affairs of the ranch would be managed by a single trustee. W. T. was that trustee until he died, and, although the three heirs all served on the board, they were powerless to affect the management of the ranch. After W. T.'s death, his widow Ella was the trustee for many years.

One problem with W. T.'s extensive lands in north-central Texas was that they had a scarcity of water. There was no aquifer beneath the land. Texas, and the entire country, had oil on the mind after the gusher known as Spindletop blew in 1901. But W. T. wasn't interested in oil—at least not at first. He wanted water. There is a perhaps apocryphal story that W. T., always looking for water, had an experimental well dug near the town of Electra one day, only to have oil fill the hole. Disgusted, he threw down his rags and said something to the effect that he didn't want the damned oil; he wanted water. He reportedly used the oil for cattle dip, diluted with water, and gave it by the barrel to townsfolk.

The real oil boom for the Waggoners began in 1911 when an oil well a couple miles north of Electra came in and appeared capable of producing fifty barrels a day. It blew during the night, and by daylight oil was gushing a hundred feet into the air. A rider went through the town of Electra yelling that oil had been found, but the townspeople at first thought it was a joke. He persisted, and people took him seriously. Within minutes, the town, which had been crowded for a trade-day event, was empty as people went on foot, on horseback, and in wagons to check the well.

The town of Electra boomed overnight. People poured into town from all over, living in hastily built shanties and even tents. The town could not accommodate the numbers, and nearby Wichita Falls began a shuttle service. Oil fever had hit Electra. W. T. still preferred his cattle, although he finally seemed to realize that the motor age was upon him, bringing a growing demand for gasoline products and lubricating oil.

Oil pools continued to be discovered around Vernon and Electra throughout the teens, but W. T. resisted drilling on his property. When pushed to lease land, he grumbled, "They leave my gates open. I've got to think about my Herefords." Albert and Electra Wharton were the first to lease oil rights on their Zacaweista land. A group of Fort Worth investors, including Amon Carter, bought leases on 78,000 acres of Zacaweista.

Amon G. Carter

Amon G. Carter, publisher, entrepreneur, and civic booster extraordinaire, was born in Bowie, Texas, and quit school at eleven. He went to work selling chicken salad sandwiches to train passengers in order to help his family's finances. Some said his mother made the sandwiches, but others suspected that the chicken was really rabbit that the teenager felled with a slingshot.

His rise in the newspaper world was rapid. By 1905, he was advertising manager of the *Fort Worth Star*; by 1908 he had purchased his rival paper, the *Fort Worth Telegram,* and merged it with the *Star.* Today the *Fort Worth Star-Telegram,* now owned by

Amon Carter, pictured holding a cigar and wearing a Shady Oaks hat, undated.

McClatchy, is the city's only daily newspaper. In the years after WWII, the newspaper had the largest circulation of any newspaper in the South, with subscribers throughout West Texas and in New Mexico and western Oklahoma. Fort Worth's first radio station, WBAP, was an offshoot of the newspaper. In 1948 it became the city's first television station.

A booster of air travel, among many other things, Carter persuaded Southern Airlines (now American Airlines) to move its headquarters to Fort Worth and worked to bring the aeronautical plant (now Lockheed Martin) to the city. The airline's current headquarters are located on the former commercial airport known as Amon G. Carter Airfield. The runway is today a boulevard named—you guessed it!—Amon G. Carter Boulevard.

Amon Carter was an enthusiastic supporter of the city of Fort Worth. It was, he claimed, where the West begins. Dallas, the rival city forty miles to the east, was "where the East peters out." So intense was Carter's loyalty that if he were forced to go to Dallas, he carried a sack lunch; he would not spend a dime in Dallas.

Important visitors to Fort Worth, including his friend Will Rogers, were lavishly entertained at his Shady Oaks ranch on the edge of the city and left wearing one of the famous Shady Oaks Stetsons. Privately and publicly, he was a larger-than-life storyteller, gambler, and drinker. His reputation was national, and he was featured in *Time,* the *Saturday Evening Post,* and other publications. He used this notoriety to bring business to his beloved city.

Carter's name is on streets, schools, a museum, a football stadium, and many other structures in Fort Worth and throughout Texas. The main entrance plaza at Texas Tech University and the main auditorium at the A&M Law School are both named for him, as is a peak in Big Bend National Park. The YMCA's Camp Carter in Fort Worth bears his name and so does a small lake near the city of Bowie, his hometown.

Carter and W. T. had a friendly financial rivalry. Many of the projects that bear Carter's name, such as TCU's stadium, were ones for which he solicited W. T.'s financial support. When Waggoner quipped about Carter getting his last dime, there was more than a little truth behind joke. The two frequently placed bets on the horses at Arlington Downs. Once, W. T. won $20 from Carter, while Carter won $25 from W. T. W. T. still used checks signed "D. Waggoner and Son," a sentimental tribute to his father, and he wrote a check on that account and asked Guy to deliver it. When Guy reminded Carter that he owed $20, the other man said, "You tell your father I'm going to frame this check and keep it as a souvenir. He may do the same with mine."

As the town of Electra had experienced an oil boom in 1911, so did Vernon when the first test well on the Zacaweista came in. Freight trains and passenger cars unloaded oil men and supplies, and men slept on cots any place they could find shelter. People opened private homes to take in the fortune-seekers. Lease prices soared. W. T. finally recognized that drilling was inevitable, but he kept three hundred thousand acres free of leases. As Porter wrote, the Roaring Twenties glittered for the Waggoners—with black gold.

Always thinking ahead, it didn't take long for W. T. to grow discontent with leasing oil rights. When he saw oil companies manufacturing crude oil into gasoline, he established his own refineries and marketing system and bought a fleet of tank cars. Pipelines transported the oil from his land to Wichita Falls and connections with several large pipelines. Eventually W. T. built a plant for mixing natural gas and improving the quality. He even owned a string of gas stations, each with the Three D logo displayed.

Oil wealth or no, W. T. remained a cattleman at heart. He complained about the greasy derricks and trucks that rumbled across his land, drivers that left his gates open. Every piece of equipment on his various oil-related properties was painted with the Three-D brand. Douglas has pointed out that in W. T.'s Fort Worth skyscraper office, the walls were lined with photographs of horse and cattle, but there was not one of an oil derrick.

Gradually, the Waggoners became city dwellers, moving to Fort Worth. Cicily Waggoner, Dan's widow, still lived in Fort

W. T. Waggoner in middle age, undated.

Worth. Electra and her husband, Albert Wharton, were the first of the third generation to make the city their home. They lived in an elegant mansion, called Rubusmont or Thistle Hill. Some say the home was a wedding gift from W. T., who wanted to keep his only daughter from moving to Philadelphia, her new husband's hometown; other sources, including the *Fort Worth Star-Telegram*, indicate Albert and Electra Wharton bought the property and commissioned the design of the mansion. Most people, however, accept the legend that building the house was a clever ploy on W. T.'s part. Electra and Albert sold their home in 1911 to cattleman and real estate mogul Winston Scott. The Whartons moved to the ranch, even though the rest of the family was in Fort Worth. For the next few years, they divided time between Zacaweista and the senior Waggoners' home on Summit in Fort Worth, often giving that as their residence address.

In 1912, W. T. began construction of a second home on Summit Avenue. Situated on three lots backing down to the river, the new home was of custom-made red brick, with white carved stone trim and an expansive, covered front porch. Behind the home were a five-car garage and servants' quarters.

The home's interior was spacious and elegant, with a marble foyer, ceiling-height fireplaces of imported Japanese tile, mahogany paneled walls, and hardwood floors. The second floor had five bedrooms and two sleeping porches. As was the fashion in large homes in those days, the wide hall served as a sitting area. The house had a primitive air conditioning system—large fans that pulled air over great blocks of ice. And in keeping with W. T.'s distrust of banks, though he himself owned banks, there was a hidden room for storing money. W. T. purchased the home next door to his, perhaps so he could control who became his neighbor. He later sold that home to E. Paul and his wife, Helen. Guy also lived in the city with his second wife and second son.

In 1923, W. T. and Ella moved to a mansion in the new and exclusive Rivercrest area in Fort Worth, and E. Paul and Helen moved into the Summit house. They stayed there until 1928, when E. Paul chose to return to the ranch. Then Guy moved into the Summit home. Unfortunately, it was among many cattle baron mansions demolished to make room for commercial progress in the late twentieth century.

While the Waggoner empire was established with businesses and homes in the smaller cities of Vernon and Decatur, W. T. apparently thought it was time to do more than live in Fort

W. T. Waggoner Building, Houston and Sixth Streets, Fort Worth, undated.

Worth. Fort Worth had no skyscraper, and W. T. decided he would build one. He enlisted Fort Worth's premier architectural firm, Sanguinet and Staats, noted for designing steel-framed skyscrapers. In that day, a skyscraper was between sixteen and twenty stories, made practical by the successful development of commercial elevators. At first, W. T. asked Sanguinet and Staats for plans for a sixteen-story building, but then he told them to go for twenty stories. The completed building boasted an ornate entrance, a vaulted bank lobby, and an elevator. It was the tallest building in the Southwest. Porter attributes the increase in height to W. T.'s claim that Fort Worth newspaperman and civic booster Amon Carter agreed to rent the top six floors. The W. T. Waggoner building was completed in 1919, with the deed in Ella Waggoner's name.

Once settled as urban dwellers, W. T. and Ella Waggoner soon became involved in civic affairs and generously supported many philanthropies. W. T.'s contributions were often coerced by Amon Carter. A picture published in the *Fort Worth Star-Telegram* shows W. T. holding up a silver dollar and quotes him as saying, "Tell Amon this is one he didn't know I had left." The photographer had been sent by Carter, only to be told that W. T., who was reluctant to have his picture taken, would not allow pictures. After some persuasion, W. T. held up the silver dollar and said, "Go ahead and shoot."

The Waggoners gave several generous donations to the Methodist Hospital (now known as Texas Health Harris Methodist), and several buildings on the Denton campus of Texas Woman's College (now Texas Woman's University) carried the Waggoner name. According to Porter, Waggoner was generous when he approved of a cause but held back when he did not. Asked to contribute to build a fence around a cemetery, he scoffed that it was unnecessary, saying he "didn't know anyone that wanted to get in there, and those that are in there can't get out."

W. T. Waggoner, holding a silver dollar that he claimed Amon Carter didn't know he had, undated.

At Amon Carter's request, W. T. sent a check to support the nomination of Texan John "Cactus Jack" Garner for president by the Democratic Party. Carter was the Democrats' national finance chairman. Waggoner stipulated that his check was neither support for the Democratic Party nor a campaign contribution but was sent because he believed Garner to be a good servant of the state. With the Waggoner contribution, Carter was able to bring the Old Gray Mare Band from Brownwood, Texas, to Chicago for the Democratic Convention.

Band members wore distinctive red silk shirts, yellow bandanas, patent leather boots, and sombreros. They were known for spreading Texas cheer and music throughout the nation, especially with their signature song, "The Old Gray Mare." In spite of this support, Garner was forced to cut a deal with New York Governor Franklin D. Roosevelt. Garner swung his votes to FDR and served as Roosevelt's vice president.

W. T. had a strict code of honor about money and his word. Once during the Depression, there was a run on Fort Worth National Bank, where he had much of his money—despite his father's early warnings about banks. Amon Carter asked him to be present as the crowd gathered so that he could reassure the investors. Carter spoke but then told W. T. that it would have more effect if he would also speak. According to Porter, W. T. told the crowd he stood behind the bank and would personally cover any losses.

A man said, "That's a fine speech, Mr. Waggoner, but would you put it in writing?" Waggoner asked him how much he had in the bank, and the man responded, "Five hundred." Waggoner turned to a banker and said, "Pay this man off." He would not stand for someone insinuating that his word was not good.

W. T. was cautious with his money, and about the only thing he ever gambled on was horse racing. If he was a cattleman at heart, so too was he a horseman in spirit. He was once quoted as saying, "A man who doesn't admire a good beef steer, a good horse, and a pretty woman . . . well, something is wrong with that man's head." Part of his ambition to be the best rancher was to own the best horses in the country.

Who knows where W. T. got his love of fast horses? It may well have been riding herd on his cattle in the early days or even racing after—or running from—the Comanche and Kiowas, but he developed an early reputation for horse racing. It was a familiar sport in North Texas, with several tracks around Decatur. Betting would start as soon as a crowd gathered, and men bet land, cattle, and horses. W. T. always had a stable of fine Thoroughbreds on his ranch, and he rarely lost a bet, though Burk Burnett was his greatest rival.

Sometime probably concurrent with the family move to Fort Worth, W. T. bought a three-thousand-acre farm south of Arlington, between Fort Worth and Dallas. There he built one of the finest racetracks in the world and kept the best blooded horses he could find. Racing, he reasoned, would encourage the breeding of better horses throughout Texas.

In 1931, he put over $2 million into the Arlington Downs racetrack on his property, gambling that pari-mutuel betting on horse races, long illegal in Texas, would be approved by the legislature. Toward that end he proposed legislation whereby a percentage of the proceeds of betting would go to the State of

Will Rogers, right, and W. T. Waggoner, at Arlington Downs on opening day of the racetrack, October 19, 1933.

Texas, to be used for the public-school fund and by the department of agriculture for the purposes of breeding fine stallions as well as general maintenance of the department's programs.

When completed, Arlington Downs had twenty stables—room for five hundred visiting horses, a large and a small track, a clubhouse (where no doubt Prohibition was overlooked), a grandstand, and a twenty-six-acre parking lot. A small lake on the grounds was home to ducks and swans, and W. T. installed a polo field. His grandson, Buster Wharton, Electra's son, was a polo enthusiast and a daring player. Guy and E. Paul managed the track with their father.

Nationally known lecturer, columnist, and comedian Will Rogers wanted to visit the racetrack while it was still under construction, and of course Waggoner was eager to show it off. The two men, introduced by their mutual friend Carter, had developed a friendship over their love of fine horses. When Rogers explained his opinion that the two men hardest hit by the Great Depression were the independent oilman and the cattleman, Waggoner replied, "Yes, and I'm both of them." Rogers knew better. When he toured the Three D Ranch, he said, "I see there's an oil well for each cow."

Will Rogers

No doubt W. T. Waggoner's friendship with cowboy humorist and social commentator Will Rogers was facilitated by Amon Carter, a friend of both men. Like Carter and W. T., Rogers had a fondness for fine Thoroughbreds and liked to visit Arlington Downs.

Will Rogers was born in 1879 in Claremore, Oklahoma, to Cherokee parents. Though he dropped out of school in the tenth grade, Rogers became known for his pithy commentaries about everything from prostitution and gangsters to politicians and the government, and for casually showing off skills he perfected as a trick roper while he spoke. He was the author of about four thousand syndicated columns, appeared in seventy-one films, performed in the Ziegfeld Follies on Broadway, and narrated countless radio programs. Rogers worked his way into American hearts with lines like, "I'm not a member of any organized political party. I'm a Democrat," or "Never miss a good chance to shut up." He often poked fun at Congress: "I don't tell jokes. I just watch Congress and report the facts," or "With Congress, every time they make a joke, it's a law, and every time they make a law, it's a joke."

An advocate for air travel and friend of Charles Lindbergh, Rogers frequently wrote about the speed and safety of airplanes and is said to have helped shape American attitudes toward the then-new mode of transportation. In 1935 he joined famed aviator Wiley Post on a trip to survey mail-and-passenger air routes in Alaska. Lost in bad weather, Post landed the plane in a small lagoon and sought directions. The plane failed on take-off and landed upside down in the lagoon. Both men were killed.

A grief-stricken Amon Carter commissioned a life-sized statue of Rogers on his famous horse, Soapsuds. The sculptor? None other than W. T.'s granddaughter, Electra Waggoner Biggs. Today the statue sits in front of the Will Rogers Memorial Coliseum in Fort Worth. Duplicates are on the campus of Texas Tech University in Lubbock and at the Will Rogers Memorial Museum in Claremore. Smaller versions were made and distributed by Mrs. Biggs, and a later casting was placed in the Anatole Hotel in Dallas.

In May 1933, Texas governor Miriam A. Ferguson signed legislation approving betting at racetracks. After the next meet at the track, track officials sent $90,000 to the state and $15,000 to the federal government. The Waggoner red, white, and blue racing silks returned to Texas tracks.

W. T. Waggoner did not see that race, though he no doubt still pocketed a handsome profit. He had suffered a severe stroke the day before the governor signed the racing bill. But by the fall season of 1934, he was in attendance, driven to the track in a long black limousine. W. T. could not see the horses, but he could hear the pounding of their hooves on the track. After a race he would ask to be driven to the stables to visit with the horses. Trainers brought them to him, one at a time, and he would stroke their noses and call them by name.

Douglas tells the story of a day when W. T.'s favorite horse, Cow Puncher, went berserk in his stall, splintering the wooden walls with his hooves and neighing as though in distress. Trainers suggested the old horse was turning outlaw, but the head groom knew better. He led the horse out of its stall and over to W. T.'s car, where the horse put his head in the car and nuzzled Waggoner. When W. T. first developed the land at Arlington, he routinely rode Cow Puncher to inspect the plant. After that first time, Cow Puncher always knew when W. T. was on the grounds, and he always demanded to visit with him.

W. T. Waggoner on Cow Puncher, his favorite horse, November 2, 1932.

In 1933, the Exchange Club of Fort Worth honored W. T. as its Citizen of the Year in recognition of his civic and philanthropic life in the city. Because of his stroke, W. T. was unable to attend, but Guy and E. Paul represented him at the banquet, where over two hundred people honored him. Will Rogers sent a tribute to be read in his absence: "Mr. Waggoner, don't take this dinner serious. It is only the beginning of a gigantic touch." He suggested Amon Carter wanted more money for this or that, and W. T. should just turn his fortune over and let Carter put him on an allowance. His message ended with, "May you live until Fort Worth can get along without you, and that means eternity."

Unfortunately, Fort Worth had to learn to get along without W. T. a lot sooner. After a second stroke, he fell into a coma from which he never roused. William Thomas Waggoner died in December 1934 and, after a small private service, was interred in a mausoleum in Fort Worth's historic Oakwood Cemetery.

He had the most land, the best cattle, and the fastest horses. W. T. Waggoner lived his life's dream, but it remained to be seen what his heirs would do with it.

CHAPTER THREE
The Next Generation of Waggoner Men

OF THE FIVE CHILDREN BORN TO W.T. AND ELLA, THREE—
Electra, Guy, and E. Paul—survived into adulthood to carry on
the family name and tradition. Electra was by far the biggest
celebrity of that generation. As Porter described her, somewhat
dramatically, "Her life had been a shining one that ignited into
a brilliant glow, then suddenly the flame went out bringing
darkness too soon." She might better be described as a meteor
that hit the earth, but her story belongs with those of the other
Waggoner women.

Both Guy and E. Paul stayed squarely within the Waggoner
tradition of cattle and horses, with an emphasis on the latter,
but neither demonstrated the ambition nor dedication of their
father and grandfather. Studies have been done on the effect
of great wealth on children. At least one study concluded that
how the children coped with wealth depended on the parenting
they received, with the implication that children whose parents
downplayed wealth grew up with a better understanding of their
place in the world. According to that theory, the responsibility
for the Waggoner children's failure to cope with wealth and the
lack of the spark that motivated their parents rests squarely on
W. T. and Ella. There is no record indicating that either W. T. or

Portrait photograph of Guy Waggoner, undated.

Ella found their children disappointing, and indeed a few references suggest that W. T., at least, was guilty of overindulgence. Various accounts show that he particularly doted on Electra I. At any rate, neither Guy nor E. Paul were as interested as their father in having the most land, the best cattle.

Guy, born in 1883, has been described as a rancher and busi-nessman. Like his siblings, he inherited one-fourth of the Three D; his was a section known as Four Corners. He and his first two wives resided in Fort Worth for a time, but he eventually built a large hacienda on his ranch land. He is known to have been on the famous wolf hunt with President Theodore Roosevelt and particularly to have helped his father with business errands and details in Fort Worth. Upon his father's death, Guy replaced W. T. as a director of Fort Worth National Bank.

A dedicated horseman, Guy was heavily involved in the operations of Arlington Downs. After W. T.'s death, Guy and E. Paul shared management of the racetrack, and Guy served as chair of the Texas Racing Commission until it was disbanded in 1937 when pari-mutuel betting was again outlawed. After liv-ing at the Three D for a number of years, he moved to a family owned property in southeastern New Mexico, called the Mos-quero Ranch or, perhaps, the Bell Ranch, principally because pari-mutuel betting was legal in New Mexico. The mansion he'd built on his Four Corners section of the Waggoner ranch stood vacant, except for sacks of grain stored on the hardwood floors by the longtime foreman who had taken a dislike to Guy. The house deteriorated to the point that it had to be demolished.

What Guy excelled at—or was a dismal failure at—was mar-riage. He married eight times, thereby establishing the family propensity toward marriage and divorce. Guy's most spectac-ular marriage was to Anne Burnett, some seventeen years his junior and heiress to Burk Burnett's Four Sixes Ranch. Burnett died shortly before the two were wed, leaving everything to his granddaughter Anne. The marriage, the first for her and third for him, combined the two largest fortunes in northwest Texas.

Rumors of impending nuptials were denied by both, even in August 1922, when they traveled, separately, to Colorado Springs and stayed at the luxurious Broadmoor Hotel. Anne's mother, Burnett's first wife, accompanied them. They married in September in New York City, with her mother as the only attendant.

The marriage was not destined to last. Guy could not resist other women and was even known to have skipped town with the leading actress from a traveling burlesque show. Burnett had given his granddaughter a strong-willed model to follow, and she was not one to sit home alone at night while her husband catted around with other women.

One night at the ranch, frustrated because Guy was again absent from home, Anne threw her things in the car and drove hell-bent for Vernon, not even stopping to open the ten gates she went through. She arrived in town with fence posts and barbed wire streaming from the car, abandoned the vehicle without even bothering to cut the engine, and left for Fort Worth.

Anne Burnett Waggoner married again, divorced, and married entrepreneur Charles Tandy of the Tandy Corporation. Sole owner of the Four Sixes, she became a leader in the livestock industry, serving on a number of boards including the First National Bank of Fort Worth, the Amon Carter Museum, the Fort Worth Fat Stock Show (now Southwestern Livestock Exposition), and the Texas & Southwestern Cattle Raisers Association.

Guy never changed his ways, marrying five more times. He died in New Mexico in 1955 at the age of sixty-seven. He had two sons by his first two wives. One son, Guy Jr., died in 1928 at the age of eighteen in a car wreck; his new bride died with him. Guy Sr. was survived by his little brother, E. Paul, who apparently had ambitions to be sole owner of the Three D and bought out Guy's widow and surviving son.

The ranch was then in the control of E. Paul and his nephew, Buster Wharton. Not many years later, E. Paul would make a move to become sole heir and would thereby add lawsuits to the family preoccupation with divorce.

E. Paul was born in 1889. Like his brother, E. Paul was a rancher and horseman. Unlike his brother, he was married to one woman for fifty years. In "Showdown at the Waggoner Ranch," Gary Cartwright described E. Paul as a "whiskey-drinking,

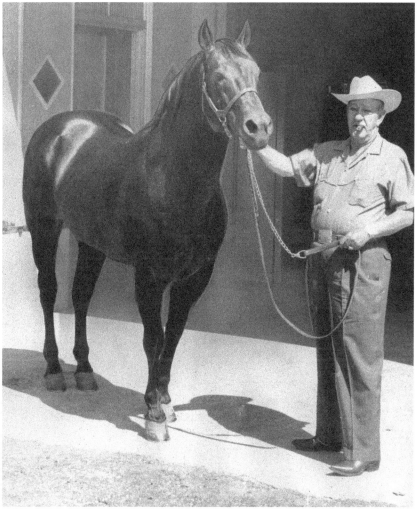

E. Paul Waggoner with his famous stallion, Poco Bueno, son of King, one of the founders of the Quarter Horse breed.

poker-playing party animal." A gentleman who knew him well recalled a "big belt buckle, expensive boots, and a bottle of whiskey." E. Paul, he said, had a good eye for horses, but he wasn't much of a rider and only rode in parades.

E. Paul had a great chance to ride in parades at the annual Santa Rosa Roundup, which he started in 1946 at the rodeo grounds in Vernon. He was part-owner of the facility. That first rodeo featured wooden chutes, professional cowboys, and a parade. The event still occurs every June, and not much has changed, though the grounds have been updated and the number of participants increased. The Santa Rosa Palomino Club has a large presence at the rodeo.

When the Waggoner Estate bought the old Methodist Church property in Vernon, E. Paul had the parsonage moved to the Roundup grounds, where it became his private hideaway. He called it Knott Inn and said the name meant exactly what it said—if you weren't invited, he wasn't in. The hideaway was the site of numerous all-night poker parties. He kept his hunting dogs and his pet monkey there, and for a while, a lion cub given to him by a traveling circus.

E. Paul had two claims to fame. The first was that he established the Three D's outstanding Quarter Horse program headquartered at his Whiteface section on the ranch. In 1945, E. Paul bought a yearling called Poco Bueno to add to his two foundation sires. Poco Bueno became perhaps the best-known Quarter Horse of all time. Waggoner bought him for $5,700 at an auction in San Angelo, Texas, after first seeing the horse at the Texas Cowboys Reunion Horse Show in Stamford, Texas. In 1947, Pokey, as he was affectionately called, was Grand Champion Stallion at the Denver National Western Stock Show and went on to victories at Kansas City, Fort Worth, the Texas State Fair in Dallas, and other arenas. After being named American Quarter Horse Champion in 1951, the horse had a distinguished career as a cutting horse. Pokey sired several champions before

Helen Buck Waggoner, wife of E. Paul Waggoner, November 6, 1930.

his 1969 death. At E. Paul's request, he was buried standing near the gate of the Three D Ranch.

E. Paul's second claim to fame was as the father of internationally known sculptor and celebrity Electra Waggoner Biggs. E. Paul married Helen Buck Waggoner in 1910, and Electra (sometimes referred to as Electra II) was their only child. Though their marriage endured, it was apparently not always smooth. Rumors persisted that E. Paul had mistresses in Mexico and South Texas. When he and Helen were apart, as for instance when she was in New York with Electra, he wrote passionate letters about how lonely he was and how glad he would be to have them home again. However, the letters were typed by his secretary.

E. Paul died in 1967 with his dream to own the entire ranch unfulfilled. His daughter inherited his portion.

Tom Waggoner Wharton

Electra I had two sons by her first husband, Albert B. Wharton. The elder son, Tom Waggoner Wharton, born in 1903, left little footprint in his brief life. He died in 1928 at the age of twenty-five, some say in a car accident, while others claim it was from syphilis. Married the first time at nineteen, he left behind eight wives but no children—in its own way, a remarkable record.

Buster Wharton

The second son of Electra I and Wharton, Albert Buckman Wharton II, was born in 1909. Known as Buster, he inherited his mother's share of the ranch, which would become half with his Uncle Guy's death, and the buy-out of Guy's surviving son. Buster didn't care one bit about cattle, but like the other men in the family, he was a horseman. His passion was polo, not racing. He was also a playboy, noted for hobnobbing with celebrities and often bringing them to his section of the ranch, where he had built a polo field, a skeet and trap-shooting range where he and friends shot live pigeons, and a landing strip.

Buster even scrabbled together a polo team out of ranch cowboys—some sources say it was called the El Ranchito Polo Club, while others cite it as the Wichita Falls Polo Club. E. Paul was irritated that Buster used the ranch cowboys that way, and that he used ranch vehicles to transport his horses. In truth, E.

Paul was probably generally irritated that he had to share his inheritance with Electra's progeny.

Buster maintained the family tradition of getting married but not staying married. He married four times (some sources say five), producing only one son, A. B. "Bucky" Wharton III.

Bucky Wharton was raised by his mother in Albuquerque and not considered part of the Waggoner line of descent—until his father, Buster, died, and he and his mother surprised everyone by laying claim to Buster's half of the estate.

PART II

The Waggoner Women

CHAPTER FOUR

Ella Halsell Waggoner

In December 1922, the Waggoner family hosted an elegant reception in the Crystal Ballroom of Fort Worth's Hotel Texas, honoring the family newlyweds. Guy had just married Anne Burnett, and Electra had taken her second husband, Weldon Bailey. In *Thistle Hill*, Roze Porter described the Waggoner women this way:

> *The Waggoner Women added to the splendor of the occasion. Ella Waggoner wore a glittering gown of black chiffon over embroidered, flesh-colored charmeuse. Helen Waggoner looked lovely in a mauve chiffon glittering with rhinestones and crystal beads. Her headdress was a diamond-studded bandeau. Electra . . . wore a handsome black and gold cloth gown with drapes in front and jet trimmings. Her coiffeur was completed by a high amber comb. Anne, youthful bride of Guy Waggoner, wore a picturesque frock of white chiffon velvet in a true bouffant style with hand-embroidered beaded flowers.*

Descriptions that could be straight out of a novel by F. Scott Fitzgerald and were certainly worlds away from the plains of North Texas and ranching life. How far they had come in one generation.

For Ella Halsell Waggoner, the journey from prairie cabin to Crystal Ballroom took a little over forty years, but in cultural terms it was an enormous leap. Born in a prairie cabin where the threat of Comanche and Kiowa raids was a part of daily life, she lived to see skyscrapers dot the skyline of Fort Worth, including one her husband built and gave to her, and to see jet airplanes cross the sky.

When W. T. called for her in his buggy and whisked her away for a wedding in Denton, Ella was not unfamiliar with ranching life in Texas. The Halsells became a prominent ranching family—especially her brothers Electious and Ewing. Ella's nephew, Harry Halsell, memorialized prairie life in the mid-nineteenth century in several memoirs, most of which were versions of the same book, *Cowboys and Cattleland,* given new and various titles and self-published. Some of his stories, while not directly affecting Ella, speak eloquently to what their lives were like.

In his memoir, Harry recalls that in the late 1860s, when Ella would have been almost ten, Wise County had between a hundred and 150 residents. Maybe thirty families lived in Decatur, and there were two or three stores. Both Ella's family and Harry's lived outside town but within about two miles.

One day young Harry was sent, with his older brother Oscar, to Decatur to fetch flour. The boys dawdled, as boys will, so it was late in the day when they were about to cross an open field on the way home. Five or six Indians came charging out of the woods. The boys fled. Young though he was, Oscar was smart enough to angle toward the woods, having calculated he could outrun the Indians. He yelled for Harry to follow him, which Harry did with speed and concentration. "No Roman soldier ever followed the Eagles more faithfully, no American ever followed the Stars and Stripes more earnestly, than I followed that white shirt tail." Once in the woods, the boys could follow pig trails through the thickets, trails that Oscar knew by heart because exploring them was his daily adventure. It being dusk, it was dark enough in the woods that the Indians couldn't find them, despite the fact they wore white shirt tails. About all young boys wore in those days were shirt tails and precious little else. They arrived home without the flour, which had scattered in the woods, and with Harry's shirt tail torn to shreds.

Harry's fear was not unusual in North Texas in the late 1860s. Every child on that prairie feared being kidnapped by tribes almost as much as they feared being killed and scalped. The stories were all around them.

Harry knew, and undoubtedly Ella did too, of the Huff family. Raiders broke into the family's house, killed a son and the mother, and left a nursing baby who was found a day later by neighbors. The kidnapping of the Babb children, Bianca and her brother Dot, was much talked about, too. Three years after they were taken, a trader reported seeing the children in a native village. The father ransomed his children and brought them home, but people knew that they had adapted to indigenous ways.

Ella Halsell lost a brother to the Comanche. Her older brother, George, left home in his late teens to ride for the Waggoner Three D, alongside Tom (W. T.). In Harry's version of the story, it was 1866 and George Halsell and Pete Harding were riding line out of a remote camp, coaxing cattle back to the middle of the range. They stopped to water their horses at a small lake, their backs to the hills. Suddenly, Indians charged over the hill toward them. George was on a fine horse, but Pete Harding had a slow pony and begged George not to leave him. George returned to his side, but George's horse began to rear, upset by the commotion. While his attention was on the horse, a Comanche shot George in the back. He tried to get away, but the warriors caught him, killed him, and scalped him. That gave Pete time to escape. In a frontier irony, the man whose life George saved later died in a barroom brawl.

Men died in saloons so frequently that when a death was announced, people asked, "Which saloon?" This death rate may speak to liquor or idleness or rage left over from the war.

Ella's father, Electious Halsell, was not a cowboy, but a quiet and mild man who ran the first (and for a while the only) tavern in Decatur. Harry described his grandfather as having a melancholy disposition and said he was often seen walking alone. He was an unlikely man to run a tavern, but his tavern was the first permanent building in the small community of Decatur. Ella, one of eight children, took her turn helping her father in the tavern, but she much preferred to work at home with her mother and younger siblings, even if it meant digging in their vegetable patch. The tavern was the daily hangout of men with nothing better to do, some of them veterans embittered by the War of Northern Aggression. Others were simply embittered Southerners, often looking for a quarrel. Harry called them "sweaters around town." Ella prayed that her father, always a pacifist, would remain silent when the men groused. Harry tells the story of the time a group of men, led by one who had lost an arm in the war, threatened Electious and went so far as to put a noose around his neck.

Electious's wife, Elizabeth Halsell, was a fine businesswoman and a true and faithful Christian with steadfast convictions as to right and wrong. But when her husband's life was in danger, she arrived with a loaded shotgun, almost immediately followed by Harry's father, also armed. The hanging was off, but the same group of men did hang five or six men, on one tree, just outside of town. Harry said it ever after gave him chills to ride by that tree.

Life for Ella's family was simple and hard. They lived in log cabins. Harry described his family cabin as a double log house with a hall down the middle and two rooms on either side. In many cases that hall was open, and the house was called a dog trot cabin. These cabins were built of straight oak logs, hewn down on two sides to create smooth walls. The ends of the logs were finished and dove-tailed, and the spaces between logs chinked with slivers of green wood or daubed with a mixture of lime and sand. Neighbors pitched in to help with the building, and it took about five days to finish a cabin.

The families ate plainly too. Corn dodgers—squares of corn-bread that had been fried, baked, or boiled—were a staple of the diet, and flour biscuits were a Sunday treat since flour was hauled in from a distant town only once a month. There was no white sugar, only brown or what today would be called raw sugar. Deer and turkey meat were plentiful, and the meat of wild hogs sometimes found its way to the table. Harry described fishing by stirring up the water until the fish retreated into frog holes in the bank. Then he and Oscar would reach in and pull out the fish—until the day Harry pulled out a water moccasin.

Ella, being a girl, more likely spent her days cooking, doing the laundry, and digging in the garden. Laundry would have been done with lye soap, made by boiling ashes with hog fat. It was unforgiving for the skin.

Decatur being the small community it then was, the Wag-goner and Halsell families undoubtedly knew each other well, and it came as little surprise to anyone that W. T. carried Ella off to Decatur to be married and thereafter took her to Dan's ranch, east of Decatur. Ella and W. T. shared a home with Dan and her sister, Cicily. W. T.'s stepmother was now also his sister-in-law.

Ella was not a memoirist, not a woman who kept a jour-nal, and more's the pity. There is little reliable record of her life between marriage and her move to Fort Worth. Those years can be partially pieced together from Porter's book, which unfor-tunately is neither documented nor indexed. We do know that those were the years that W. T. was building his dream to own the most land and the best cattle in the country. He and his father grazed large herds at several North Texas locations and bought new land aggressively, which meant that both men were often gone from the ranch. The threat of Comanche and Kiowa raids vanished like a bad dream, due primarily to Quanah Parker settling his people on the reservation in Oklahoma. Still, Cicily and Ella, left alone on the ranch, were probably never truly alone but guarded by a contingent of Waggoner cowboys.

In the early 1880s, Dan Waggoner decided to move his family to Decatur and built El Castile. While it was no longer advised to cluster in communities for protection, Dan may well have had the education of his grandchildren in mind, along with a sense that they would fare better in life if their experiences were not limited to the isolation of ranch life.

Apparently, W. T. and Ella did not immediately move to town with Dan and Cicily, but they were surely established in El Castile when their children were still young. For all that she was raised on the prairie and lived in a fairly remote and small Texas community, Ella Halsell Waggoner was a woman of the Victorian era. We sometimes mistakenly associate Victorianism with noble women in England who wore elaborate clothes and spent their days at teas and balls or reading, embroidering, or playing the piano. That was not Ella's life, but she still had a clear vision of the proper role of women and what she wanted for her only daughter.

Electra seemed content in Decatur, with frequent rambles across the prairie with her father in his buggy. It was Ella who wanted the girl to have an education and arranged for her to spend three years at an exclusive "finishing" school in Tennessee. Finishing schools in those days emphasized manners and cultural matters and prepared young ladies for a life of social activities. One suspects that Ella, having moved from a small prairie cabin to a mansion, albeit still in Decatur, saw an upward trajectory to her life and wanted to secure that same pattern for her daughter. That may have been her big mistake. The Waggoner children, however, were not indulged as youngsters. They took part in community activities and made firm friends in Decatur.

Roze Porter recounts the story of the time the circus came to town, and the Waggoners, like everyone else, turned out to watch the parade. Except no one could find young E. Paul—until he came down the street with the parade, proudly leading an elephant. Daniel yanked his grandson out of line and gave him a swift kick in the pants for such a dangerous stunt. E. Paul was said to have still stung about the incident years later when he told the story to a reporter for the *Fort Worth Star-Telegram.*

By 1900, the Dan Waggoners had moved to Fort Worth, leaving Ella as the mistress of El Castile. She supervised a massive redecoration of the home, including the now-famous fresco murals painted and signed by an artist named Donecker. Fresco was the technique of painting watercolor on wet plaster so that the plaster absorbed the color. For the ceiling of the El Castile parlor, Donecker created a garden of flowers and vines that radiated from the central chandelier.

By 1902, Ella would be grateful she had the work done, as she prepared for Electra's elaborate wedding and the teas, showers, and luncheons that preceded it. The year 1902 was momentous for the Waggoners in another way. Daniel Waggoner, the family patriarch, died, and his loss dramatically changed the family structure.

By 1905, W. T. and Ella were still living in Decatur, although he was serving on the board of First National Bank in Fort Worth and undoubtedly had other business interests in the city. The two grown Waggoner children—Electra and Guy—were living in Fort Worth. Ella and W. T. soon followed them, establishing a residence at 530 Hill Street. Young E. Paul was away at school. W. T. always claimed his business interests necessitated the move to the city, including the Waggoner Bank and Trust, of which Electra's husband was second vice president and Guy was cashier. But no doubt the pull of family exerted an influence—and perhaps social consciousness.

In 1906, the *Fort Worth Star-Telegram* ran an article about the number of cattle barons who maintained homes in the city or owned property there. Fort Worth was built, the newspaper claimed, by cattlemen and their interests. The article listed twenty-some who had bought homes in the city, including such names as the Reynolds brothers of Lambshead Ranch, Clarence Scharbauer of the Panhandle-based Scharbauer Cattle Company, and Winfield Scott, who would later buy Thistle Hill, the mansion built for the Waggoners' daughter, Electra I. Cattlemen owned much of the downtown area, with Winfield Scott owning the most property. Included among those who owned a good bit of property was the widow Mrs. Dan Waggoner. Separately, the newspaper listed a 1906 transaction whereby W. T. purchased the home on Hill Street (now Summit Avenue).

W. T. soon bought and subsequently built for his wife what would for a short time be the grandest mansion in Fort Worth. Located at 1200 Summit, the home was squarely within the boundaries of Quality Hill, Fort Worth's upscale community on the bluff above the Trinity River. There, in an area roughly a square mile, wealthy families seemed to vie with each other to build the most lavish and luxurious homes. The area was bound by the river to the west, Henderson Street to the east, Seventh Street to the north, and Pennsylvania Avenue to the south. Downtown was just east of Quality Hill.

The people of Quality Hill brought diverse backgrounds and sources of wealth. There were, as mentioned, several cattle barons who maintained residences there, especially those with land nearby. Some spent the week on the ranch and the weekend at their city home. But there were also bankers and real estate men, railroad executives, and a few cotton kings. To live on Quality Hill was a mark of wealth and social prominence. It was to see and be seen.

These diverse people had one big thing in common: they all had wealth. And they lived a lifestyle appropriate to that wealth.

Young boys went to boarding school or military academies; young girls went to finishing schools. For both, education was often "finished" off with a grand tour of Europe, from which they brought home a taste for all things European, from décor to dress. Accordingly, the homes of Quality Hill did not feature cowhides and horns but Victorian interiors, with drapes and floor cushions and ornate furniture and wall patterns. One home boasted a "wicker" room with furniture that today would be assigned to a porch.

Quality Hill women did not do their own housework. Indeed, with the lavish style of entertaining and frequent house guests who stayed for days, that would have been almost impossible. Hard as she worked as a youngster, Ella put that life behind her. Like their neighbors, the Waggoners had a staff of household servants and yard men, with someone to look after the horses and carriage. By then W. T. mostly got about in a carriage.

Ella would have found herself with interesting neighbors. Major K. M. Van Zandt, a Fort Worth pioneer and prominent banker and civic leader, was an early resident of the enclave, having built an elaborate Victorian home at 800 Penn Street in the 1880s. Widowed twice, Van Zandt had three wives and fourteen children, and his home site included room for homes for several of the children. One son eventually built a more modern house adjacent to his family home.

Many on the Hill had national and international connections. Frank Weaver, one of the original owners of Fort Worth's Panthers baseball team, lived on Penn Street, in a mission-style mansion built for banker Otho S. Houston. Weaver's daughter, Katherine Weaver Rose, was known as an opera singer and traveled extensively in Europe, where she was almost marooned by World War I. Katherine once dated Guy Waggoner briefly. Apparently, she was one woman he did not marry.

Charles Silliman was president of the board of trade and manager of Land Mortgage of Texas, a company of English investors. Like several neighbors, Silliman kept farm animals on his property—a cow and some turkeys.

Joseph B. Googins and family occupied an unusual house, the first floor of stone and the second of slate, with a tile roof, and a swimming pool in the basement. The third floor had the traditional ballroom found in many of his neighbors' homes. A Chicago native, Googins was manager of the Swift Packing Plant on the North Side and was a good family friend of Marshall Field of Chicago department store fame. The Googins' daughter later married Elliott Roosevelt, son of Franklin Delano Roosevelt.

The rancher W. T. knew best, Burk Burnett, beat him to Fort Worth, buying the Ball property at 1424 Summit for his second wife, Mary Couts. Burnett remodeled and dramatically changed the exterior of the elaborate Queen Anne structure, also adding tennis courts and a pergola.

Ella Waggoner may have liked finding herself with such powerful and interesting neighbors—certainly her grown children did—but she kept a low profile. Known for holding her emotions in check, she outlived two of her three grown children. She was present when Electra died, but newspapers tactfully did not allude to Ella's mental state. One imagines she remained outwardly composed, though caught up in an inward storm.

When Guy died in Vernon in 1950, she was said to have broken down once in the company of a good friend. Ella was in Fort Worth, her house filled with grieving friends come to comfort her. She sat straight, looked them in the eye, and thanked them, all without shedding a tear. But when Etta Turpin, wife of stock farm manager Glenn Turpin, arrived, Ella shooed everyone away, politely of course, so that she could collapse in her good friend's arms and weep unconsolably.

If she was not a social butterfly, Ella was probably an underappreciated businesswoman. Her part in advising W. T. on ranch and business matters was never publicly exhibited, but Porter records one time when she appeared piqued at not being kept in the loop. W. T.'s original plans called for his skyscraper, the Waggoner Building, to be sixteen floors. With encouragement from the architectural firm of Sanguinet and Staats, Waggoner chose to extend the building to twenty floors. One day, in conversation with Ella, he let that fact slip.

"You went to twenty floors without telling me?" she asked. Readers may use their imaginations for her tone of voice.

From the time of W. T.'s death in 1934, until the mid-1950s, Ella was the sole trustee for the estate. Under the terms of the Massachusetts trust that governed the estate, that position gave her the final word on all matters involving the estate. That means she made the decision to reduce the Fort Worth presence that W. T. had established and move the estate headquarters to Vernon. She oversaw construction of the headquarters building at Vernon, which many saw as a tribute to W. T. The building is square and solid and was, in its day, the height of luxury, with conference rooms and individual offices on the first floor. A large photograph of W. T. dominated the general conference room on the second floor. A VIP dining room on the second floor was decorated in an Oriental theme and furnished with antiques. The building represented a sharp contrast to the line camps and dugouts from which Dan and W. T. had built their empire of the biggest ranch with the most cattle and the finest horses. Ella also approved the request, made by Guy and E. Paul, to sell the stock farm in Arlington.

Ella administered the estate and oversaw these advances, large and small, from her Fort Worth home. After W. T.'s death, she also demonstrated her business acumen in real estate matters. She sold the Rivercrest house and built another one but sold it when the roof collapsed while she was in bed sleeping. She lived in an apartment in the Hotel Texas until she purchased her final home at 1200 Hillcrest. Ella Waggoner resigned as trustee of the estate in favor of E. Paul at some point in the mid-1950s. By then, Guy was dead, and she was in her nineties.

Mrs. W. T. Waggoner, June 4, 1939.

As she was a careful businesswoman, Ella was a bit parsimonious, perhaps because of the early habits of her lifetime. Electra Biggs, who called her grandmother Mammy, as did many others, once recalled that when she asked Mammy's cook to bake her favorite cake, Ella worried about the amount of sugar required. (It could have been during wartime rationing, but Mrs. Biggs did not specify the year). Ella also hired a new companion who happened to like her coffee in equal parts with cream. When Ella saw her use almost an entire pitcher of cream one morning, she instructed the kitchen the next day to put only a bit of cream in the bottom of the pitcher.

When Electra, married and mother of one infant with another on the way, asked her grandmother to provide a window unit air conditioner for her New York apartment, Ella replied, "Air conditioners are unhealthy. Get a fan."

Ella lived with a companion, a housekeeper, a maid, and a chauffeur who drove her 1940 Packard. The chauffeur frequently tried to get her to trade her car for a newer model, but she refused to spend the money.

Shortly after her ninety-ninth birthday, Ella became ill and spent the last year of her life bedridden, her hearing and sight failing. There was no celebration for her hundredth birthday, and she died shortly afterward. Pictures supplied by the family for the book on Thistle Hill show a remarkably beautiful woman in middle age but one who grew progressively more solemn in appearance, especially with an increasingly severe hairstyle, and one who shrank as she aged. The unknowing person, seeing her on the street, would have been unlikely to recognize her as a person of wealth and power.

But Ella Waggoner had lived a remarkable life, from the prairie cabin and the tavern in Decatur to the exclusive Rivercrest neighborhood in Fort Worth. Just as the estate building in Vernon may be seen as a pinnacle, Ella may be seen as pivotal in bringing her family from ranch to city. W. T. established his headquarters in the city for business reasons, but he built his Summit Avenue mansion for Ella. One suspects she wanted to be near to her grown children, all three of whom lived in Fort Worth for varying periods of time. But it is not difficult to imagine the move to Fort Worth as part of Ella's plan for her family's life, a grander step but still one related to her insistence that Electra go to finishing school.

We can only wish that Ella had kept a journal of events and her interpretation of them, her feelings and emotions over a long life that spanned almost half of the nineteenth and twentieth centuries. The world changed in amazing ways during that hundred years, and apparently, so did Ella Halsell Waggoner.

CHAPTER FIVE

The First Electra

Born in 1882, Electra Waggoner could be said to have burst forth from a cocoon with her 1902 marriage to Albert Buckman Wharton. She certainly moved into a wider world, with a world tour, followed by the move to Fort Worth as a newlywed. Over her relatively short life, Electra developed a reputation for extravagance. Since she was a carefree woman who smoked, drank, occasionally indulged in "unladylike ways," and generally enjoyed her freedom from the restraints of society, it is tempting to picture her as a typical flapper from the Roaring Twenties. But Electra's party years occurred at the turn of the century, twenty years before WWI, Prohibition, and flappers. The mores of society were still there—Electra just often chose to ignore them. Such behavior was not unusual for daughters of the wealthy at the time, but Electra lived her life so flamboyantly that she became at least a regional sensation.

Electra Waggoner was the second child in her family, named after her maternal grandfather, Electious Halsell. The name "Electra" comes from classical mythology and a tangled tale of incest and murder. As the daughter of Agamemnon and Clytemnestra, Electra helped her older brother, Orestes, murder Clytemnestra and her lover in retaliation of the murder of Agamemnon. In a somewhat contradictory message, the name connotes a brilliant, magnificent beauty. Electra briefly became an only child when her older brother Dan died in December 1882; Guy and E. Paul were born shortly thereafter and rounded out the family.

From the first, W. T. doted on his daughter. He took her on rides on his ranch holdings in his wagon and taught her to ride—a pinto pony at first and then his Thoroughbreds. The ranch cowboys called her the Little Princess of the Panhandle.

Her earliest years may have been spent on the ranch, but Electra essentially grew up as a town girl. Many small towns have that one "princess," the girl who is the child of the richest family in town, and Electra was undoubtedly that child after her family moved to Decatur. She and her brothers were not isolated from town life but rather were active participants in it. Electra had a group of friends and one best friend—Ada Cates. The next-to-youngest of ten children, Ada often visited El Castile, the Waggoner home, perhaps seeking refuge from her large family. She also frequently accompanied Electra on trips to the ranch.

Electra was only fifteen when she was sent to the Ward Seminary for Young Ladies in Nashville, Tennessee. The finishing school, founded in 1869, was considered one of three top institutions for girls in the nation. It later merged with Belmont College to become Ward-Belmont College. Electra is not listed among the distinguished alumni, for whatever that means. By happy coincidence, Ada, known for her musical ability, attended Centenary College in Cleveland, Tennessee, to continue her musical studies. W. T. and Ella escorted the girls to Tennessee on the train. For three years, Electra would only return home for summers and holidays.

When she moved back home in June of 1900, Electra had already begun her move into the wider world. From all reports, the meaning of her name, "magnificent beauty," was now apparent. She had light brown hair, fair skin, blue eyes, and all the social graces. Soon part of a group of girls who called themselves the Merry Makers, she was at the center of a whirlwind life of parties and teas. The girls often gave parties to which they invited young men from the area. One such party was a tea with an elaborate Japanese theme. El Castile was decorated with hanging lanterns, fans, and Oriental flower arrangements. As hostess, Electra wore a kimono. Apparently, an admission fee was charged, for it is recorded that "benefits" went to the Young Men's Social Club.

Another of Electra's parties, this one for girls only, required that guests come in costume. About half the ladies wore outfits from the Napoleonic era, while others came in gowns from America's early years, a la Martha Washington and her contemporaries. During this period in Decatur, Electra learned social lessons that would later serve her well in Fort Worth and Dallas when she entertained frequently, often large numbers of people.

The round of parties in Decatur was punctuated by trips to the ranch with Ada, shopping trips to Dallas, excursions to Bowie and San Antonio, a visit to Fort Worth's Fat Stock Show, and even a trip to Denver. On all these outings, Electra and the other girls were well-chaperoned, but they still found a new freedom in their social lives.

Many young men were entranced by Electra—after all, she was young, beautiful, and wealthy. But she had one special beau, Max Lingo, who was in the lumber business in Dallas. In 1901, Max proposed, and Electra accepted, but apparently W. T. and Ella did not like the match—or the young man. They persuaded their daughter to go on a world tour before settling down to marriage. Electra agreed but assembled her trousseau before traveling, so that the wedding could be held soon after her return.

By 1900, it was again fashionable—and safe, European wars having quieted—for young, wealthy people to go on grand tours before settling down to the business of life. The custom began in the seventeenth century when young men went abroad for two or three years. The thought was that exposure to the wider world, including art, culture, and the roots of civilization, added the finishing touch to education and prepared young men to take their place in society. The custom died out in the early nineteenth century, mostly due to unrest in Europe, but was resumed after the end of the Napoleonic Wars brought peace.

Undoubtedly, Electra was well chaperoned on her tour, but there is little record of who accompanied her and no record of the sites she visited. We do know that South Asia was on her itinerary because she apparently met her future husband in Nepal. And she clearly spent time in Austria, for she brought home a wedding veil of antique rose point Austrian lace. Her tour was shorter than those once advocated for young men, and by November of 1901, she was back in Decatur, where she shocked and titillated the Merry Makers by revealing a butterfly tattooed on her leg. She also described, at length, a man named Albert Buckman Wharton, whom she traveled with after they met in the mountains of Nepal. The engagement to Lingo was off. Without her itinerary, it is impossible to know if she purchased the veil before or after she met Albert. Which bridegroom did she have in mind—Max or Albert?

Albert Wharton was described as a handsome blueblood from Philadelphia. Today, he has no internet presence to supply his background or breeding, but we can surmise that he was related to a respected and well-known Philadelphia philanthropist named Joseph Wharton, who had made his fortune as an ironmaker and later banker. He was a cofounder of Bethlehem Steel and Swarthmore College and endowed the Wharton School of Business at the University of Pennsylvania. Joseph Wharton had three daughters and no sons. Two of the daughters married, one to a member of the Lippincott family of publishing fame, and took their husbands' names. The third daughter never married. So, while Albert Wharton could not be a direct descendant of Joseph, he was quite likely either a nephew or grand-nephew or otherwise connected to the prestigious family.

Electra and Albert were married June 10, 1902, at El Castile. Ella and Electra were kept busy in the months leading up to the wedding with showers, teas, and luncheons in honor of the bride-to-be. El Castile had to be cleaned and polished until it shone. Electra was no doubt even more appreciative of the fresco decorations after her European experience. There was also lavish food to prepare.

Shortly after the wedding, the couple left on an extensive European tour. Plans called for them to settle in Philadelphia upon their return. Stories conflict as to how they ended up in a mansion in Fort Worth. A widely accepted legend claims that W. T. did not want his only daughter so far away and thus purchased the old Zane-Cetti estate in the Quality Hill area of Fort Worth. (Jesse Zane-Cetti was a well-known Fort Worth civic leader and founder of the Texas Brewing Company, which produced beer and ice and, years later, Tee Total Beer.) The "honeymoon cottage" was to be W. T.'s wedding gift to the couple.

But the *Fort Worth Star-Telegram* reported that A. B. Wharton (they variously called him E. B. and George) bought the land for $25,000 before the couple left on their honeymoon and hired the architectural firm of Sanguinet and Staats to draw up the plans—the firm that would later design several Waggoner mansions in the city as well as W. T.'s skyscraper. In reporting on the purchase, the newspaper said Wharton had extensive livestock interests around Decatur and was reported to be a millionaire. Construction on the house did not begin until the newlyweds returned from their European trip.

The Whartons lived at El Castile while their Fort Worth home was under construction, but Wharton soon found himself embroiled in a legal battle. He had fenced the Fort Worth property, thereby closing off an alley. Neighbors objected that they needed that access and took him to court. Since everyone involved was prominent in Fort Worth, the case garnered much public attention and speculation. Porter records that Wharton gave the city a strip of land to be used as an alley.

There were other milestones in Electra's life, though none perhaps as significant as her wedding. Still, not every wealthy socialite has a town named after her. The town of Beaver was also known as Waggoner Switch, since the railroad had been extended to a special switch point for W. T. to load his cattle. In 1902, residents were tired of their split identity and wanted to settle on one name. They preferred Waggoner, but W. T. did not want the town to use that name, so they voted to call it Electra. Today the town has a population of about three thousand and claims the title of Pump Jack Capital of the world.

The other significant event in Electra's life was the 1903 birth of her first son, Tom Waggoner Wharton, who arrived while his parents were still residing at El Castile. The Whartons and their infant son moved into their Fort Worth mansion in 1903. Electra called her new home *Rubusmont,* a French or Latin term meaning "Thorn Mountain." It became generally known as Thistle Hill.

Thistle Hill, Electra's honeymoon "cottage," had eighteen rooms, six bathrooms, and about eleven thousand square feet. Despite its size, the term *cottage* was appropriate in the day. The word often indicated a second home, and it may have implied that Electra's primary home was still on the ranch, even after her marriage. The term may also have indicated the informal, Colonial Revival design of the house, with wood trim rather than limestone or wrought iron.

When first built, the mansion stood alone on a slight rise in the ground and dominated the scene around it, positioned so that it would catch any summer breeze. The only other permanent structure on the property was the carriage house, no doubt built to Wharton's specifications to hold both automobiles and

Water tower behind Thistle Hill, 1509 Pennsylvania Avenue, Fort Worth, the "honeymoon cottage" of Electra I and A. B. Wharton.

horses. Unusual at the time, it had a gas pump and storage tank, as well as a pulley system for loading hay to an upper storage area and releasing it as needed to the horses. An adjacent cooling yard provided space for walking horses. The property had a signature water tower of green shingles painted to match the roof of the house, with a white balustrade. A well house, adjacent to the kitchen, had open lattice-work walls painted green, again to match the house roof.

Consistent with the Colonial Revival style, the house boasted two-story wooden pillars on the front porch, which, with a wooden balustrade, encircled the front of the house. The main house was brick with a wood shingle roof and two dormer windows.

Electra filled the cottage's eighteen rooms with art treasures, many of which she had brought from abroad. Guests entered through a leaded glass doorway with an arched fanlight above. That semicircular motif was found throughout the house. Inside, a large reception area was dominated by a massive horseshoe staircase with a wide lower portion that rose to a landing with a three-part Palladian window—a large arched central portion, flanked by two smaller windows, almost certainly by Tiffany. The staircase then divided into two smaller staircases that led to the second floor.

Electra most likely decorated this foyer with tables holding photographs and knick-knacks, a piano, perhaps urns and bronze figures, and several chairs. Radiators provided heat in the chilly months. To the left was the drawing room, a stiff, elegant room with delicate furniture, used only on rare and highly formal occasions; to the right, a library that was probably a gentleman's retreat with leaded glass bookcases and dark walls. The first floor also had a dining room, a small solarium, and a small morning room, plus a kitchen roomy enough for several servants.

One of the most interesting rooms was the game room, directly behind the library. Likely used for billiards and card

The grand staircase in Thistle Hill, 1509 Pennsylvania Avenue, Fort Worth, the "honeymoon cottage" of Electra I and A. B. Wharton.

games, its wide plate rail, more suitable for trophies than plates, and its massive fireplace suggest it was perhaps intended for display of Wharton's dog trial and horse racing trophies.

The second floor offered a large, open seating area at the top of the stairs, with the master bedroom, a sleeping porch, and boys' rooms to the right, and guest rooms to the left—the bird's eye maple room and the mahogany room, with tiny, corded beadwork outlining the woodwork.

Thistle Hill's third floor is a puzzle—one large room that may or may not have been a ballroom. In all probability, the Whartons used this as a party room but rarely if ever held formal balls. There are also two small servants' rooms on the third floor.

If this seems like overblown opulence for a girl from a North Texas ranch, it must be remembered that for all but the first few years of her life, Electra had lived in a fine mansion, albeit one smaller than her honeymoon cottage. Still El Castile had its own touches of elegance, especially after the fresco paintings were done. Again, it is possible to trace Electra's taste for elegance and glamor to Ella Halsell Waggoner's aspirations for her only daughter.

Electra did not wait long to move into the social scene in Fort Worth. The 1903 social announcements in the newspaper told of an informal luncheon for Guy's current wife. The newspaper called it "one of those delightfully served affairs, delicate and delicious."

The Whartons were soon entertaining lavishly. What happened in the mansion on the hill was big news in Fort Worth. There was a 1906 Halloween "phantom dance" to which guests wore pillowcases and sheets; the only lighting came from glowing pumpkins. That same year Electra arranged a candy pull in the kitchen and an al fresco party on the porch where guests played card games and watched vaudeville performers. An evening billed as "L'espagnol" followed a Spanish theme, and a New Year's open house for 160 guests saw the ballroom "elaborately decorated with smilax (a climbing vine once widely used for decoration) and tinsel and a large Christmas tree." Another New Year's the open house in the afternoon was followed by a supper for seventy. On this occasion, the ballroom was a "bower of vines and roses." Not all entertaining was done in the couple's home—a barbecue at Handley was reported or a party at the Natatorium, the city's indoor swimming pool.

The *Fort Worth Star-Telegram* frequently carried small notices that Mrs. Wharton had issued invitations for this or that event—an al fresco card party, a Valentine's dance, a luncheon for two hundred, dinner at the Country Club. Evidently social consequences were not considered in announcing such invitations. Were those left out not piqued? Did those included flaunt their social status? Frequently, a short piece labeled a news article would report simply, "Mrs. A. B. Wharton spent Monday in Dallas." She appeared to go to Dallas often.

Through all this, Albert Wharton was a shadowy, mysterious figure. Ever the proper host, he was at his wife's side when they entertained, and he had a certain prominence in the city as owner of the first automobile agency. He even organized the Fort Worth Automobile Club in 1904. Wharton's other interests were horses and dogs. He kept horses as well as cars in the carriage house at Thistle Hill and had his own personal kennel, though it is not evident that it was on the grounds of Thistle Hill. Interested in field trials, Wharton attended a meet of the U.S. Field Club with dogs from his kennel of blooded bird dogs on at least one occasion. He was among the few dog owners listed in an article pointing out a scarcity of good hunting dogs—there were more sportsmen than dogs.

The Automobile in Fort Worth

When Electra's first husband, A. B. Wharton, opened his Fort Worth Auto and Livery, it was the first such agency in town. An article in the July 23, 1899, issue of the *Fort Worth Register* heralded the reign of the automobile, citing the machine's many advantages. "The old equine favorite is passing away. The electric gong of the automobile has sounded his death knell."

Despite the *Register*'s enthusiasm, not everyone embraced the automobile. Their noise and speed frightened horses, and merchants were angry when horses bolted, sometimes causing damage. People claimed that the excessive speed of automobiles was a hazard to pedestrians. Still, Wharton saw increasing sales.

Most automobiles in the day were water-cooled, which involved hoses and radiators. They had removable curtains for comfort in the winter and a match holder for lighting the headlights. Customers provided their own toolboxes, which usually included a pick, shovel, and wire cutters, the latter for cutting through fences to avoid obstacles in the road or cut across fields for shortcuts. Doubtless, farmers were not impressed. Drivers wore white dusters, a cap, goggles, and gauntlets for the necessary protection of the hands from hot metal.

Wharton sold Wintons (a four-passenger, single cylinder, eight horsepower vehicle with a water-cooled engine designed by Scotsman Alexander Winton) along with Franklin automobiles (a four-cylinder model with an air-cooled engine). Franklins were considered luxury cars, on a par with the Buick or Packard, both of which appeared on the market much later.

In addition to gasoline-powered engines, Fort Worth streets saw traffic of cars powered by steam and electricity. But gasoline was the most popular.

One of Wharton's ads for his agency suggested that cattlemen park their horses at his livery and rent one of his cars while in town. Like Winton, Wharton saw racing as crucial to the success of the automobile. A racing park was established west of downtown Fort Worth, and at a 1906 meet, Wharton drove against legendary driver Barney Oldfield. There is no record of who won. The Fort Worth newspaper reported every time A. B. Wharton left the city to participate in an automobile race—and that was frequently. He entered some speed competitions but seems to have been more interested in distance contests.

The new *Fort Worth Star-Telegram* advocated for the auto by sponsoring endurance races to West Texas, such as a 1906 race that went from Dallas to Fort Worth to Abilene and San Angelo and then returned by way of Brownwood and Stephenville, a five-hundred-mile loop.

By 1910, there were 959 registered automobiles in Fort Worth, and the city hired its first motorcycle officer. The speed limit in town was seven miles per hour. The officer's duty was to catch speeders, and he laid out a speed trap on West Seventh Street, west of downtown. The officer rode an Indian Motorcycle that no doubt came from Wharton's agency. Guy Waggoner was among those cited for excessive speed.

Automobiles also led to litigation. Architect Marshall Sanguinet was taken to court after a resident accused Sanguinet of killing his dog in his speeding automobile. Wharton was called in as an expert witness. He testified that if Sanguinet was in second gear, as he claimed, he could not have been going as fast as the plaintiff said. In another instance, Wharton himself was charged after his car hit a Western Union messenger. "Automobile Accident—Smash-Up with a Trolley" was a large headline in the *Star-Telegram* in another instance.

In addition to cars, horses, and dogs, Wharton also apparently tried his hand at real estate. It was reported that he had bought property at the corner of Seventh and Throckmorton, with the intent of erecting an apartment building to be called the Sloan Building (no record of why that name was chosen). It was to be complete with a grill and café, but for some time the newspaper reported that Wharton was still working on his plans. Eventually he sold the property at a profit, leading one to suspect he was doing a bit of speculating. He apparently owned and sold several smaller houses in the area and probably owned a cluster known as the Wharton cottages. Still, when the newspaper listed cattle barons who had moved to Fort Worth, they included Wharton among them.

In 1905, Electra got her own automobile, the first electric car seen in the city. The car was called a lady's automobile with a "delicate" five-horsepower engine. The red-and-black vehicle seated two and would be useful for "going shopping, to the theatre or to church." Electra was described in the newspaper as an "excellent automobilist" who could be seen "whizzing noiselessly along the streets . . . in perfect control of her machine."

Electra was no doubt a leader in fashion as the introduction of automobiles dictated some changes in women's clothing. Women's hats were smaller and tilted forward, to avoid being blown off, though they still sported feathers and flowers. But the dust kicked up by the machines on dirt streets and roads necessitated veils to protect the face and gloves for the hands.

In spite of the social whirl, Electra did not spend all of her time in Fort Worth. She took frequent trips to the ranch, often with a companion in tow, and occasionally visited St. Louis. As a couple, the Whartons spent summers in Colorado Springs, where they had a cottage. One year, A. B. was stricken with paralysis while in the Springs and hastily returned to Fort Worth, where it was reported that he had improved to the point he could walk from the train to a waiting automobile. After a period of recovery, he was seen driving about town again. The public diagnosis was altitude sickness.

Electra and A. B. welcomed their second son, Albert Buckman Wharton Jr., in 1909 while they resided in Thistle Hill. In between the two boys, Electra lost a baby girl to miscarriage.

Thistle Hill was burglarized at least twice while the family was vacationing in Colorado Springs. Valuable apparel, rifles, shotguns, pistols, and sporting equipment were taken. A young man who worked for a paving company eventually confessed to the crime and led police to his loot. Another time, prowlers broke in a back window and apparently fixed themselves an elegant lunch and then napped on a couch. Nothing was taken, and police theorized the burglars were scared off before they could gather cut glass, silver, and jewelry.

The most serious robbery at Thistle Hill proved to be an inside job. Electra kept her jewelry in a secure safe, but one Tuesday night, when she had worn some valuable pieces, she put them in a jewel box in her bedroom rather than returning them to the safe. The next afternoon two jewel boxes were discovered missing—one held rings and broaches, and the other held A. B.'s personal jewelry, such as studs, rings, cigarette case, and a watch. The total worth was estimated at $7,250. Police arrested Electra's personal maid and the butler, though the latter was released. The maid, however, proved to have several aliases and a history of jewel theft. It was suspected she had an accomplice in Philadelphia to whom she shipped the goods.

With the 1909 distribution of the Waggoner estate to Electra and her two brothers, the Whartons decided to sell Thistle Hill and move back to the ranch. They sold the mansion to the Winfield Scotts for $90,000. It was one of the largest real estate transactions for residential property in the Southwest. The Scotts undertook serious remodeling of the home, changing the exterior to the more formal Greek Revival style, replacing wooden decorative elements with iron, replacing the shingle roof with imported green tile, and putting limestone columns on the front entrance where there had been wooden columns.

Scott was a self-made millionaire, with extensive real estate holdings in Fort Worth and elsewhere. Born in Kentucky and raised in Missouri, he came to Texas at the age of twenty-one when, it was claimed, he chopped wood for a living and could neither read nor write. He returned to Missouri to marry his childhood sweetheart, but she died after a year, leaving him with a daughter, Georgia Townsend. He then married Elizabeth Simmons, a physician's daughter from Weatherford, Texas. At the time he purchased the house, he and his family, including ten-year-old Winfield Jr., were living in St. Louis where Scott was president of the East St. Louis Oil Mill Company. He announced, however, that the family would return to Fort Worth, where his holdings included the Mutual Cotton Oil Company, four hotels, and several other downtown properties. Unfortunately, Scott died while Thistle Hill was being renovated, and Mrs. Scott moved in as a widow, with her son.

Thistle Hill Today

Today, Thistle Hill sits in the middle of Fort Worth's hospital district. Known as Fort Worth's castle, it is the best and almost last surviving mansion from the Quality Hill and cattle baron era. It is owned by Historic Fort Worth, serves as a museum, and is available to rent for weddings and other special events.

The house has had a checkered history.

The Scotts' son, a black sheep, blew through his inheritance and sold the house in 1940 to the Girls' Service League, a philanthropic organization that provided homes for underprivileged young women.

The Girls Service League, struggling for funds, had neither the money nor the interest to preserve the house—preservation did not become a popular topic until the 1960s. The condition of the house deteriorated. But if the league had not occupied the house, it would have been vacant and fallen into severe disrepair even faster. By 1968, there was less need for housing for young girls, and the league could not undertake the improvements required by long periods of deferred maintenance. They offered the mansion for sale, and only two outcomes seemed likely: it would be demolished and the property commercially developed, or the building itself would be turned into commercial use.

A loosely organized group of citizens without much historic preservation skill came together in an organization known as Save-the-Scott. Though they worked to maintain the building, their main focus was on fund-raising to allow them to purchase the site. Several times it seemed their efforts were in vain. Finally, in 1976, Save-the-Scott got the keys to what was known as the Scott house. They immediately restored the name Thistle Hill and began the restoration process.

It was not surprising that during reconstruction, several ghost sightings were reported—a woman, dressed in white, who appeared on the dramatic staircase landing, and a man in tennis clothes with a handlebar moustache. Workmen reported music floating from the third-floor ballroom, and others reported odd footsteps and voices, even a rocking chair that was mysteriously moved and then returned to its original spot. There have been no reported sightings in recent years.

The Whartons meanwhile divided their time between El Castile in Decatur and Zacaweista, Electra's portion of the ranch. Electra oversaw construction of a home on high ground, surrounded by oak and pecan trees. It was, she once said, her Christmas present to herself. The two-story stucco structure welcomed guests with two horseshoe hitching posts in front. The name "Zacaweista" was spelled out in tile on the exterior. The house sat on one side of what was called "the square," facing what today amounts to a small village with a bunkhouse, a couple of houses for a foreman and married cowboys, a cookhouse, and sheds. Buster, Electra's son, later added a stone barn for

Stone archway of the entrance to the Zacaweista Ranch headquarters, seventeen miles south of Vernon, Texas. The gate is dedicated to W. T. Waggoner, who died in 1934.

training his polo ponies, and in 1965, Tony Hazelwood, long-time foreman, was buried in the open area in the center of the square.

Wharton, having apparently sold his automobile agency, devoted himself to the ranch and cattle, although his name appeared frequently in real estate news and court proceedings in the Fort Worth paper. A 1910 article began, "Mr. and Mrs. A. B. Wharton, millionaires . . ." and detailed their half-million-dollar purchase of the Park Hotel in Dallas. But all was not well with the Whartons' marriage.

According to a January 27, 1921, article in the *Dallas Morning News*, $3 million worth of property was at stake when Electra

Waggoner Wharton filed for divorce, ending her eighteen-year marriage. Electra moved to Dallas, one assumes without A. B.

Stories conflict about the purchase of Shadowlawn, Electra's Dallas estate. The *Fort Worth Star-Telegram* reported that Mr. and Mrs. A. B. Wharton purchased the elegant property, then about a year old, but the *Dallas Morning News* attributed the purchase to Electra alone. Shadowlawn was a seven-acre Dallas estate complete with its own lake. Electra spent $90,000 remodeling it and another half million furnishing it. She filled her home with art and antiques, such as a Persian carpet valued at $42,000; a banquet table and matching inlaid Venetian cabinets; and an imported marble chest. It was said that it took fifteen coats of paint to get just the right shade as she redecorated.

While many surrounding mansions have been demolished, Shadowlawn survives today at 4700 Preston Hollow Road. It is Georgian in style, more elaborate than Thistle Hill but strangely reminiscent of her first home because of two-story pillars on the front porch. Electra only lived at Shadowlawn a year and a half.

In both Dallas and Fort Worth, newspapers still referred to Electra as Mrs. A. B. Wharton. As the newly appointed chair of the Texas branch of the Women's Roosevelt Memorial Association, Electra was responsible for raising money for a memorial to the recently deceased Theodore Roosevelt, and she was often in the papers hosting fund-raising events. She also planned a reception honoring former senator Joseph Weldon Bailey, who represented Texas in the House and the Senate, ran unsuccessfully for governor of Texas, and later died in a courtroom in Sherman, Texas. Newspapers offered differing reports as to the number of guests anticipated. One report was ten thousand, which likely would have stretched the capacity of even Shadowlawn and Electra's hospitality. Another more conservative report was that a thousand were expected. The event was canceled at the last moment because of a conflict in Senator Bailey's schedule.

After the divorce, A. B. was rarely mentioned in Fort Worth or Dallas papers. His name still appeared occasionally in reference to court proceedings or real estate transactions. Gradually, A. B. disappeared from public notice, and he may well have returned to Philadelphia.

If anything, Electra's entertainment became more lavish after her divorce. She hosted national politicians, movie stars, and international socialites. Guests at Shadowlawn were served such delicacies as grouse, breast of guinea, stuffed pheasant, and hothouse strawberries in January. They dined on fourteen-carat gold and sterling silver dinner services. Parties often lasted until dawn. Her delight was to invite eastern dignitaries and show them a bit of the Wild West—such as the time two guests shot six-shooters through the dining room ceiling. Once, she held a formal dinner party and unexpectedly packed the entire party off to Zacaweista to see an oil well gush in. Electra also traveled extensively to Europe and several American cities, making the social seasons in Washington, DC, and Palm Springs. She kept a summer home at Spring Lake, New Jersey, perhaps another "cottage" like Thistle Hill.

Wherever she lived, Electra brought elegance and extravagance to the scene. She was famous as the first person to spend $20,000 in one day at Neiman Marcus. The next day she went back for the things she had forgotten. She had fresh flowers throughout her homes every day, refused to try on clothes that anyone else had previously tried, wore the latest New York and Paris fashions, but never wore the same gown twice, and was said to own 350 pairs of tailor-made shoes.

She either traveled to New York for her clothes or had a clever Dallas seamstress copy the latest Paris fashions. She changed clothes frequently during an average day, with specific outfits for every type of party or occasion. The chemise had come into fashion, with a dropped waist, straight fit, and hem beneath the knees. Electra no doubt favored long strings of pearls and small beaded purses. Cloche hats were the rage, though no pictures suggest Electra favored the fashionable bobbed haircut.

Electra married twice more after her divorce from A. B. Wharton. Her second husband was Weldon Bailey, son of former senator Joseph Bailey. The marriage did not last, and the couple, married in 1922, divorced in 1925. She almost immediately married James P. Gilmore, a Chicago manufacturer and former head of the Federal Base Ball League, a short-lived third major league. Texas law required a waiting period after divorce, which Electra ignored, and the marriage was annulled.

Electra had lived a charmed life, with little or no diversity—going from princess of the prairie to town princess of Decatur, a European tour and a fairytale romance, a town named after her, and the birth of two sons. But in the 1920s, life began to come down hard on her. After she divorced and her third marriage was annulled, her health failed. Following the annulment, Electra took back her maiden name and moved to New York City, where her younger son, Buster, was in school. She had not been well in some time, but in November she apparently had surgery of some kind. She was said to be recovering well with a good prognosis when her condition took a rapid downturn. Ella Waggoner was with her daughter and took her to a hospital.

When Guy Waggoner heard his sister was critically ill, he tried unsuccessfully to charter an airplane to take him and his wife to New York City. He then chartered a train on the Pennsylvania Railroad. The track was cleared for him, and the train made it across the country in a record twenty hours and twenty-eight minutes. Ella, Guy and his wife, and Electra's younger son, Buster, were with Electra when she died. No official cause of death was ever made public. The romantic story was that she died of a broken heart after the annulment, but others diagnosed cirrhosis of the liver. She was forty-three years of age.

Services were held at the home of her younger brother, E. Paul, and she was interred in the family mausoleum in Fort Worth's Oakwood Cemetery.

Describing her as a beautiful flame too soon extinguished seems a bit overdramatic for a life essentially spent in self-indulgence. But it seems equally simplistic to point out that succeeding generations often fail to live up to the standards and accomplishments of highly successful people—the families of Churchill, Franklin Roosevelt, and Rockefeller come to mind. Perhaps W. T. and Ella overindulged their children, especially with the 1909 distribution of land and cattle. Electra's contribution to her world rested primarily on bringing glamor and glitz to people's lives and on producing two sons, one of whom died young. The other son became a dedicated playboy, polo player and alcoholic, marrying four or five times.

Perhaps Electra inherited her grandfather's and father's indomitable spirit and determination to be the greatest and create a legacy. As a well-schooled young woman of that era, she had few outlets for that drive and energy. She may have expended it in the only way she knew—through a life lived in excess.

Throughout her life, Electra demonstrated yet another Waggoner trait: an affinity for more land. She was subject to its pull, returning to the family ranch frequently, even taking guests. Her sense of entertainment at the ranch was as large as it was in the city.

CHAPTER SIX

Electra Waggoner Biggs

ELECTRA II BROUGHT A NEW DIMENSION TO THE FAMILY LEG-
acy, as a successful artist, even while she fulfilled the roles of
heiress and international celebrity left to her by her aunt, the
first Electra. Perhaps even more than her namesake, young
Electra felt the pull of the land. Although she was born in Fort
Worth, lived in New York, and traveled extensively, Electra II
spent most of her adult life living on the Waggoner ranch.

The second Electra was born November 1912 in a Fort Worth
hospital, the daughter of E. Paul and Helen Buck Waggoner. Her
first two years were spent on Quality Hill, in a house close to her
grandparents' home. But then E. Paul took his family back to the
ranch, and Electra enjoyed a ranch girl's childhood. Like her aunt
before her, she was the cowboys' little princess, and they favored
her with all kinds of treasures, including baby rabbits to raise.
She went with her parents to Vernon for supplies, riding in the
open sidecar of her father's roadster—a buggy, windy experience,
as she once recalled. Occasionally they went by horseback, which
she remembered as a long ride. She and her parents often followed the chuckwagon to share in the beef and beans cooked by
the cousie or cook. On hot nights, they sometimes slept outside
under the stars.

But 1918 found her back in Fort Worth, where E. Paul purchased the house next door to W. T. and Ella, and her mother, Helen, began a private school in the family garage. It became Marsh's Private School, a fashionable school for girls. In addition, young Electra had music and dance lessons, all the trappings of an upscale childhood. Visiting her Aunt Electra in Dallas was a special treat; she played dress-up in the older woman's bountiful wardrobe.

Electra delighted in the attention of many beaus at an early age, beginning to date at twelve and soon learning to sneak out of the house. As a teen, she was sent to a boarding school in Bryn Mawr, Pennsylvania, where she knew no one and was miserable, treated as an outsider by the other girls and mocked for her Texas accent. Eventually she made friends and enjoyed her life at the school, especially because almost every weekend meant a date and a party at one or another nearby college campus. Her summers were spent in Europe, with her mother, and she soon spoke fluent French.

Electra was never a good student. She likely had the capacity but not the interest. In boarding school, she switched her major from college prep to "finishing," the courses that prepared students for social life and emphasized cultural matters. She flunked Latin after she was caught augmenting her lessons from a translation book given her by a friend. (In Porter's book, the point is clearly made that the friend was a young man named Hagman, who later married Mary Martin and was father to actor Larry Hagman—such connections mattered greatly to Electra.)

Among her many beaus, a young accountant named Gordon Bowman was special. They met on a ship to Europe after her junior year. The next spring, she was invited to his senior house party, although she didn't know that his friends invited her as a joke, and he knew nothing of the invitation. She rallied, enjoyed the weekend, and before she went back to school, they were pinned, a tradition whereby a fraternity man gave his pin to a girl as a pledge of fidelity. She saw Bowman often after that, balancing his steady attention against a string of one or two dates with others. The couple became unofficially engaged, but she continued to see many young men, and Bowman knew it. Electra made a proper debut at the prestigious Baltimore Bachelors Cotillion, but Bowman was apparently not in attendance.

Electra had a talent for getting herself into situations that would embarrass her. She went to a house party where she met a young man named Jimmy Stewart (not the famous actor). Somehow, they wandered to a small, private pool where guests were skinny dipping. Electra was horrified, but Jimmy led her back to the main swimming pool on the estate, where bathing suits were in order. In typical fashion, she always described him as a "favorite lifetime beau."

For Porter's biography, *Electra II,* Electra recalled a scary night in Paris when a young man she met, who thought she was much older than sixteen, tried to fix her up with a lesbian. Electra had rarely ever heard the word. She escaped, still innocent, and though the incident frightened her, it did not cause her to act more cautiously in her social life.

After completing boarding school, Electra moved to a residential school for young ladies in New York. As Ella had shaped the life of Electra I, Helen made every effort to shape her daughter's life. When Electra II took classes in art history, music, and Italian, her mother decided it was not enough and enrolled her in a business program at Columbia University. Every day at lunch, Electra and Gordon Bowman would go rowing, and he would do her homework. When the professor called her into his office to say that she was doing unusually well in her studies and was far ahead of her class, she confessed all. He advised her to give up accounting. Searching for something to fill her days, she dabbled in sculpture—playing with clay, she called it—at Miss Katherine Breeze's Studio. She gained enough skill that she knew how to build an armature, and she had a bit of confidence about her work.

The Depression years didn't bother the Waggoner family, and Electra danced the nights away and slept until noon. Reading Porter's biography, one can almost hear Electra's voice, reeling off the names of young men who courted her—Winthrop Rockefeller among others—and the places she went—the Waldorf Astoria, the Biltmore, the Roosevelt, the Plaza, the Ritz. Life in the early 1930s, for Electra, was a round of teas, luncheons, and dances. She knew the leaders of all the big-name bands as personal friends—Eddie Duchin, Guy Lombardo, and others.

One band leader was special—Enrique "Enrico" Madiguerra, a native of Spain and a violinist who had studied with Jascha Heifetz, stole her heart. Her family had a fit. E. Paul hired detectives and finally came to New York, gun on his hip, threatening to kill Enrico and every member of his band. Helen took a more temperate approach but kept Electra practically a prisoner. In retrospect, a reader of the story might well wonder if Electra was in love with Enrico or with the intrigue of a forbidden passion.

She gave in to family pressure and agreed to marry Gordon Bowman. Nothing was spared in planning for an elaborate wedding to be held at the Waldorf Astoria. Edward Steichen did her wedding portrait, which later appeared in *Vogue* magazine. Her gown was designed by one of Hattie Carnegie's designers, and she wore her aunt's antique, imported rose point lace veil.

Sometime before the wedding, Electra went, with Helen's blessing, on a blind date to accompany another couple she knew. Her date was an attractive man named John Biggs. She may not have remembered him, but he remembered her, and (knowing nothing about either Enrico or Gordon Bowman) he swore he would marry her. He was surprised—and angered—when he received an invitation to the wedding.

Electra II in her wedding gown.

John Biggs

John Biggs, the man who wooed Electra away from a stable of beaus, was born in Sherman, Texas, one of five children. He attended public schools and did his college work at the Virginia Military Institute, a school so traditional that it excluded women until 1997.

John Biggs, manager of the W. T. Waggoner estate at the headquarters in Vernon, Texas, January 19, 1953.

Electra, who always described him as a man's man, said he would have disapproved of VMI's decision to include women. He was both a scholar and an athlete, graduating first in his class and having led baseball and football teams.

After graduation, he was offered one thousand dollars a month to play baseball for the New York Giants but was also offered a management training position with the International Paper Company at one hundred dollars a month. After soul searching, he chose the executive future offered by the paper company. His salary explains the inexpensive nature of his first date with Electra. She recalled years later that he would occasionally stay up all night playing bridge and poker to make enough to take her to "21" for dinner.

After Pearl Harbor, Biggs was on active duty with the U.S. Army, stationed in Washington, DC. He never got the overseas deployment he hoped for. After the war, E. Paul Waggoner lured John Biggs to the Waggoner Three D Ranch with the offer of an assistant manager position and director of the Santa Rosa Rodeo.

Over the years, Biggs was increasingly respected as both a rancher and a businessman. He served on the board of banks in Vernon, Wichita Falls, and Fort Worth and served a term as president of the Texas and Southwestern Cattle Raisers Association.

In the late 1960s, Biggs made a landmark decision for the ranch; he announced the disposal sale of all Poco Bueno horses. People came to the ranch from all over the world to purchase the progeny of the horse that was arguably the most famous Quarter Horse ever. Poco Bueno, aging and ill, was put down in 1969. In 1970, John Biggs retired as director of the Santa Rosa Rodeo and offered the rodeo grounds for sale. He had run the annual rodeo for twenty-four years.

John Biggs died of throat cancer in 1975 and was buried in the Waggoner Biggs family plot in Sherman, Texas, with his wife, mother-in-law, and father-in-law. They are watched over by the sculpture of an angel, created by Electra.

Amid details of planning for the wedding, Electra continued clandestine meetings with Enrico. The night before the wedding, he begged her to run away with him. Her sensible side won, they parted ways, and she married Bowman. She didn't love him, but the consolation was, in her mind, that he adored her. Helen was pleased; Electra was not.

Electra and Gordon Bowman were married in June 1933 at St. Bartholomew's Church. She was twenty-one. E. Paul walked a tearful bride down the aisle and, at the last minute, told her they didn't have to go through with it. She continued down the aisle.

From the honeymoon on, the marriage was a disaster. Gordon was sick for the entire honeymoon. They returned from Canada to stay with his parents until their apartment was ready. Unknown to Electra, her mother-in-law had furnished the apartment with heavy, dark furniture and hired an Irish maid who disliked Electra but adored Gordon. Gordon left her alone while he worked long hours and then he went hunting, so she continued her affair with Enrico, which perhaps shows what you can get away with when you have money.

Thinking his letters would reach Electra when he was in Monte Carlo with his band, Enrico sent them to her mother. Helen, however, did not share them with her daughter. Instead, she took Electra on a cruise and arranged for her to go ashore at Monte Carlo, with a young man they met onboard the ship as an escort. Helen, knowing that Enrico was in Monte Carlo, reasoned that he would see Electra in the company of yet another man. He did, and always a jealous lover, he wrote a bitter note ending their relationship. Helen was pleased; Electra was devastated.

The story advanced to all the elements of a romance novel—a suicide attempt, an estrangement, and finally divorce. Electra and her mother spent six months at a Nevada dude ranch establishing residency for a quickie divorce. Of course, there were some cute cowboys on the ranch.

Electra, reportedly thin and rundown, took her broken heart from Reno to Los Angeles to recuperate. She was soon out and about, meeting such celebrities as Bette Davis, Conrad Nagel, and Dick Powell. She even had an unsuccessful screen test, after she met a talent agent. At a party, she saw a sculpture and, recalling her play with clay in New York, remarked that she could do that. Almost as a lark, she modeled a bust of a young man she knew and gave it to his parents. It marked her return to sculpture.

After a Christmas spent in Fort Worth, where her parents were living in the Hotel Texas, she went back to New York determined to polish her skills in sculpture. She still spent evenings dancing and mornings sleeping, but now she spent afternoons working in a studio. The "godfather of young American sculptors," W. Frank Purdy, an elderly man by then, encouraged her, saying that she had talent and with perseverance she could do well at the art.

Prohibition had been repealed, and "café society" blossomed in New York. Electra frequented "21," El Morocco, and the Stork Club. The list of young men courting her was long, and she partied every night. But at the suggestion of a family maid, who had heard through the maid grapevine that John Biggs clearly remembered her, she called John Biggs, whom she barely recalled from the blind date before her wedding. With his limited finances, he took her to Coney Island on the subway for their first date. Thereafter, they dated regularly.

Fort Worth's Amon Carter, good friend of her grandfather, commissioned Electra to do a sculpture of Texas politician Vice President John Nance (Cactus Jack) Garner for the 1936 Texas Sesquicentennial. Garner refused to pose, so Electra spent hours in his DC office, watching and studying, waiting for him to emerge from behind his newspaper. Eventually she completed the bust from photographs, which were easier to get along with. The sculpture was unveiled in Texas at the 1936 Texas Centennial celebration in Fort Worth. Carter ordered several castings of the Garner bust and commissioned her to do a similar bust of his friend, oilman Sid Richardson.

Summer found Electra and her mother again in Los Angeles, where one columnist wrote: "Having failed to find happiness and contentment in being one of the richest girls in the world forced blond Electra Waggoner Bowman of Fort Worth, Texas into a studio loft in New York where, within a year, [she] had hewn a successful career for herself in the world of sculpture." Calling her the Doris Duke of Texas, the article claimed she saw art as a livelihood, not just an escape for the "poor little rich girl" dilemma.

With subsequent commissions, she proved her dedication. Spotting actor Victor McLaglen in a restaurant, she told friends he had the kind of good, strong face she'd like to sculpt. She then boldly walked up to him and asked if he was interested. He was. The two rode horseback every morning at six because he had been ordered to lose weight for the film he was working on, *The Magnificent Brute*. Electra lost weight after their rides; McLaglen did not. The sculpture was unveiled at the premiere of the movie and remained on display in New York's Roxy Theatre for the duration of the film's run. To celebrate, Electra took a group of friends to the Stork Club for dinner and then to the Roxy.

Other commissions followed: Notre Dame's Knute Rockne, Frank Phillips of Phillips Petroleum, a memorial plaque in tribute to W. T. unveiled at his beloved Arlington Downs. She worked hard on a head of her maid, a woman of African American and Native American heritage. Eventually that piece, carved in black Belgian marble and called "Enigma," won third place in the prestigious Salon d'Automne in Paris. That Paris honor reflected the results of a summer of study at the French Valsuani foundry where she learned to cut marble and cut the "Enigma."

Electra's first major exhibition opened in April 1938 at the Seligmann Galleries in New York, with thirty-one pieces. Hav-

Bronze bust of vice president of the United States and native Texan John Nance Garner, December 14, 1945. The bust, made by Electra Waggoner Biggs, was presented to Texas Technical College (now Texas Tech University) by Amon Carter, chair of the first board of directors for the school.

ing an opening there was a real coup and tribute to her career. The gallery was founded in 1880 in Paris and was among the most prestigious in New York. During the three-week show, all available pieces were sold, including some medallion portrait pieces on which she had been working with the help of Mr. Purdy, who used the Lincoln penny to teach her about engraved images. Her cousin Buster and his current wife were among her portrait subjects, and they traveled from Texas to attend the opening. Electra was surrounded by reporters, art critics, and photographers. "Enigma" sold for $3,000 to the European gentleman who had wanted to buy it before it was entered in the Salon d'Automne.

Electra immediately went to work on several new commissions—a series of panels depicting the history of lighting, commissioned by Consolidated Edison, and a bust of Amon Carter Jr. Amon Sr. remained a big supporter of her work and gave her the next big advance in her career. He commissioned her to do a life-sized statue of the late Will Rogers on his beloved horse, Soapsuds. Rogers, a close friend of both Carter and W. T., had been killed, along with pilot Wiley Post, in a plane crash in Alaska in 1935.

Electra began work on the sculpture, working in the California barn owned by Rogers's son, Jimmy, and using the actual horse, Soapsuds, as a model. The work was hard—the barn was hot, and the flies unbearable, but she created a ten-inch clay model. In August, she took the model East and worked in the Boston studio of sculptor Arnold Geissbuhler, who taught at Wellesley and whose work was noted for both realism and abstractionism. With the teacher's guidance, she created a four-foot working model of the sculpture, which was submitted to Rogers's family and friends for approval. Then came the life-sized version.

Meanwhile, Electra was preparing portrait pieces for an early 1939 showing at the Paul Flato Salon on Hollywood's Sunset

Photo of the Will Rogers statue, created by Electra Waggoner Biggs, just before the unveiling ceremony at Will Rogers Memorial Coliseum, November 15, 1947.

Boulevard. The opening was star-studded, and Electra was surrounded by celebrities, the life she cherished. She also prepared work for a three-day exhibition Flato held at the 1939 New York World's Fair. For this, she showed bracelets, amulets, portraits, statuettes, even a cigarette case.

Back to concentrating on the statue of Rogers, she worked at a foundry in Astoria, New York, where a walkway with a ladder had been built so that she could reach all parts of the statue. She found that at that size, all the faults were magnified, and nothing she did corrected them. She couldn't get it right. Purdy advised her to tear it down and start over, advising her no one would care how long it took. She tore it down. This time, she worked with a model, who was about Rogers's size and build and who wore Rogers's clothes as supplied by his widow. A policeman from the NYPD brought a horse as her model.

One day the policeman's wife confronted her at the studio. It seemed the policeman, bored while the horse posed, had drunk a few beers and had come home smelling like a brewery. The wife suspected some monkey business, but Electra assured her she was only interested in the horse, not the man.

The sculpture, titled "Into the Sunset," was completed, at 9'11" and 3,200 lbs., in early 1942. It was crated and shipped to Carter in Fort Worth, who stored it for five years, waiting first for his son, Amon Jr., to come home from a WWII prison camp and then for the right person to dedicate the statue.

By late 1946, Carter had the statue in place in front of the Will Rogers Center in Fort Worth, but it was boxed up to be hidden from public view. All of Fort Worth was curious, and there were several attempts to tear away the protective boards. These attacks always occurred in the middle of the night. A hefty $5,000 reward for anyone who caught the vandals encouraged most police officers to drop everything else in hopes of being the one to collect the reward. Author Jerry Flemmons claims in his biographical *Amon* that some of Amon's own buddies at the Fort Worth Club were guilty, after a night of indulging in a few drinks, but they apparently went unpunished and probably unidentified.

By the time a bunch of high school boys tried to "get a look at Old Will," Amon had lost his patience, if he ever had any. The boys, from Paschal High School, swore each other to secrecy, but as will happen, one boy bragged to his girlfriend. She told her mother, and her mother told the police, hoping to collect the reward money. The braggart was arrested and immediately ratted out his buddies.

Amon had the boys brought to a room at the newspaper offices, where he stormed and thundered at them. Their names, he threatened, would be published in the paper, even though he had a long-standing rule against publishing the names of juvenile offenders. They would be barred for life from events at the Will Rogers Center—that would include Fort Worth's annual stock show and rodeo. Then he decided not to press charges. Nobody collected the reward, and Carter donated it to the Fort Worth Police Officers Benevolence Society.

One of those young boys was seventeen-year-old Elston Brooks, an enterprising fellow who already had his own radio program, "Ballads by Brooks." Not too long after the "statue caper," Brooks went to work as a cub reporter at the *Star-Telegram*. Over the years he worked his way up to entertainment columnist, and he and Carter talked often, but neither one ever mentioned the statue.

In 1947, with his son safely home from a POW camp in Poland, Carter decided that it was time to unveil the sculpture and that General Dwight D. Eisenhower was the man to unveil it. Electra was thrilled that Amon pulled out all the stops to make the dedication a grand affair. The Trumans and the Eisenhowers were in attendance, former Texas congressman Fritz Lanham presided over the ceremony, and Margaret Truman sang "Home on the Range." When she heard the words of praise and the cheers from the thousands of onlookers, Electra burst into tears.

Replicas of the statue were later placed on the campus of Texas Tech University in Lubbock and in Claremore, Oklahoma, near the Will Rogers Memorial Museum. A later casting was placed in the Hotel Anatole in Dallas.

One of the most difficult pieces she undertook was a bust of President Harry S. Truman. She lamented that he had no distinguishing facial characteristics, other than his ever-present glasses, which complicated a sculptor's challenge. But Bess and Margaret liked the work, and they were the critics who mattered to Truman.

With all this work, Electra kept up her active social life, dating many young men. But Johnny Biggs was the constant, the

Electra Waggoner Biggs with President Harry Truman and her sculpture of Truman, November 15, 1948.

one she saw most often. After the events at Pearl Harbor, Biggs took leave from the paper company and went on active duty with the U.S. Army, assigned to the Quartermaster Corps in DC.

For the summer of 1942, Electra rented a house in Connecticut, which was constantly filled with friends, especially her many male admirers. Descriptions make it sound like one long house party, and Porter writes, "It was a fun summer," which seems an ironic way to describe the first summer the United States was directly involved in WWII. In those days of Rosie the Riveter, the war's effects on Electra most significantly meant a fabric shortage, which dictated dramatic fashion changes.

John Biggs, who she called Johnny, got away to visit her when he could leave Washington. After that summer, Electra, still busy with her sculpture, decided she was ready to marry John Biggs. When she announced that, he tried to discourage her from the uncertainty of a wartime marriage, especially since he still hoped to be sent overseas. What Electra didn't know was that he was engaged in an intelligence operation aimed at flooding the enemy troops with counterfeit American currency. That operation would require him to travel frequently to Europe as a courier.

She persisted, and the small wedding was held on April 25, 1943, in the apartment of friends. Amon Carter attended; her parents, in the midst of marital difficulties, did not. After a brief Florida honeymoon, the newlyweds went home to John's one-room apartment, a third-floor walk-up, in DC.

Electra was in some ways unprepared for marriage—she was not a cook. Her first attempt at cooking a chicken left their apartment a mess and her in near hysterics—she had tried to clean the chicken, a necessity in those days that involved plucking pin feathers and cleaning out the insides of the chicken. Her effort to cook dinner for his boss was equally disastrous, but she did better at motherhood. Electra III was born July 6, 1944, and

Helen, April 30, 1946. By the time their children were born, the Biggs were back in a New York apartment.

After another celebrity-filled summer in Connecticut with people named Chrysler and Bouvier, among others, the fall of 1945 saw the Biggs family move back to the ranch, where E. Paul had offered Johnny the dual positions of assistant ranch manager and manager of the Santa Rosa Roundup. They lived at Santa Rosa, the Mediterranean stucco house her parents had recently built when they returned to the ranch after several years as residents of Fort Worth's Hotel Texas. E. Paul and Helen built a smaller house nearby.

Within a few years, the young heiress had made dramatic changes in her life, going from a wide and wild social life with many beaus to marriage and then from New York to a Texas ranch that, no matter how large and successful, was still the farthest thing from dwelling in the city. Surprisingly, Electra seemed content to center her life at Santa Rosa, with Johnny and her daughters. She traveled frequently to New York and DC and took her daughters to Europe when they were old enough. At the ranch, she entertained lavishly and often, and guests included Rex Allen, Michael Landon, Robert Taylor, Ken Curtis, and others. Her accounts of the poolside parties and elaborate dinners were always rounded out with mention of the men who adored her.

She continued her sculpture career, accepting both public and private commissions and having converted a guest bedroom at Santa Rosa into her studio. The best overview of her artistic accomplishments is probably the collection at the Red River Valley Museum on the campus of Vernon College. The museum's Waggoner collection includes sculptures and a model of her studio but also photographs, guns, saddles, and other memorabilia reflecting not only Electra's career but the centrality of the Waggoner Estate in the life of the region around Vernon and Seymour. Apparently, no catalog raisonné exists of her work. She

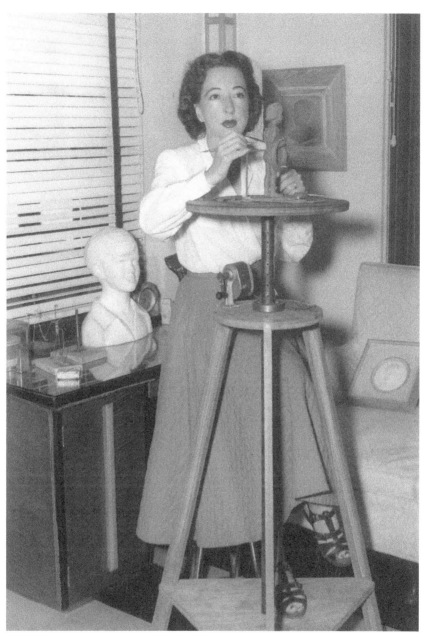

Electra Waggoner Biggs, working on a sculpture for her show to be held at the Fort Worth Art Association gallery at the Public Library, beginning January 1950.

never publicized nor promoted her pieces and never hired an agent. Commissions came to her by referral and word of mouth, which again raises the question of the importance of talent vs. connections. Electra Biggs was apparently blessed with both.

In the late 1960s, changes were underway at the ranch. John Biggs announced a dispersal sale of Poco Bueno horses, and in 1969, the great horse himself had to be put down. Per instructions left by E. Paul, Pokey was buried, standing, near the main gate to the ranch. During this time, the family also felt the intrusion of the outer world—one year while most of the ranch, owners and cowboys, were at the Santa Rosa Roundup, $100,000 worth of jewelry was stolen from Electra's mother, Helen. Authorities suspected international jewel thieves and speculated about the use of a helicopter, but the case was never solved, the jewelry never recovered. The Biggs daughters both married in the late 1960s, Electra III to Charles Francis Winston of Houston in 1968 and Helen to Gene Wade Willingham, also of Houston, in 1969.

Another big change came when John Biggs offered the roundup and its grounds for sale or lease. With the support of the local community, the rodeo association voted to continue the production. The grounds were eventually sold to be used as a brood farm for racehorses; the new owners agreed to continue the annual rodeo. As of 2019, the rodeo was still held every year.

In 1974, Johnny was diagnosed with throat cancer. After major surgery, a period of recovery was followed by metastasis to his lungs. Biggs underwent grueling months of therapy but died in August 1975, almost exactly a year after the initial diagnosis. He was buried in the family plot in Sherman, next to E. Paul and Helen, who had died in 1973. Within two years, Electra lost her mother and her husband.

Life changed after Johnny's death. Electra apparently spoke freely and often about missing him and being lonely, but she immersed herself in family life, with four grandchildren who called her Nana. Electra Winston had two daughters, including Electra IV, and Helen Willingham had a son, John, and a daughter, Jennifer. The Winstons lived first in Houston, then in Santa Fe, and finally in Florida, but Electra II was grateful to have the Willingham family close by at the ranch. They occupied the small house that E. Paul and Helen built near Santa Rosa.

Electra fulfilled some of Johnny's professional obligations, serving on the board of directors of Fort Worth's First National Bank and as an honorary director of the Texas and Southwest Cattle Raisers Association. She continued to accept commissions—a bust of Robert Justus Kleberg of the King Ranch (another of good friend Bob Haase) and a hundred twelve-inch miniatures of the Soapsuds statue that were sold before she even had them cast. In her eighties, Electra accepted fewer commissions but continued to work, especially on miniature portrait medallions, and to entertain lavishly at the ranch. For every dinner party, she worked out a menu, and then she and her cook prepared the complete meal as a test.

The most thorough account of her life is in Porter's laudatory book, which closes several years before Electra's death. There is little record of her last years, though an obituary notice from the *Vernon Daily Record*, oddly tipped into the Porter book, refers to a long illness. She died in the Vernon hospital, April 23, 2001, and is buried in the Vernon cemetery with her parents and John Biggs. Despite the wide and cosmopolitan world in which she lived, she apparently chose to die close to home and to be buried there.

She was a woman of complexity. The wealth of her family—from the empire built largely by her great-grandfather and grandfather—enabled her to live and party on equal terms with East Coast celebrities, always surrounded by a cadre of admiring men. But, unlike her aunt, she did not content herself with that life; she spent time and effort developing her artistic skills and thereby bringing a certain stability to a family reputation that had been marked by flamboyance. In a family known for an astounding record of divorces, after one brief failed marriage she married for life in what was apparently a happy union. And she returned to make her life at the family ranch, as a wife and mother, the source of all good that had been given her. She once disparagingly claimed that there was no water on the land and the oil was played out, but she stayed there. She did not abandon society, traveling often to see friends and bringing celebrities to party at Santa Rosa. But the ranch seems to have been her anchor, and she seemed destined to be the one to preserve and continue the family heritage.

Yet when she tangled with Bucky Wharton over the future of the land, Electra was the one who wanted to sell and distribute the assets, although there is no record of the influences on her by the early 1990s. Speculation is always dangerous, but without Johnny to guide her, she may have been influenced by those managing the ranch, including Gene Willingham. And during that period, there were no trustees of the estate, from whom she might have sought advice. It may be too that her health declined either mentally or physically, in her last years, coloring her judgment. If so, that is a well-kept family secret.

When Electra Waggoner Biggs died at the age of eighty-nine, Bucky Wharton, W. T.'s great-grandson, was the sole Waggoner descendent left on the ranch—except for Helen Willingham, who continued to live there. And Bucky's story is an entirely different chapter.

Electra's Imperial Goulash Recipe

Somewhere along the way, Electra II learned about food and cooking. But this recipe indicates she had help—a cook—to cube the meat and stir for three hours. It was also probably helpful, because of the quantity, that she had her own beef. This, a surprisingly straightforward dish to serve celebrities, comes straight from the pages of *Dining with the Cattle Barons*. Electra Biggs called it "Imperial Goulash."

Ingredients:

- 8 lbs. beef chuck cut in 1-inch cubes
- 1½ cups flour mixed with 1 Tbsp. salt
- ½ tsp. savory
- 1 Tbsp. pepper
- About 2/3 cup butter for browning
- 2 lbs. peeled, sliced onions
- 2 lbs. fresh mushrooms, wiped clean and sliced
- 2 cloves crushed garlic
- 1 tsp. salt
- ¼ tsp. pepper
- ½ tsp. savory
- ¼ tsp. oregano
- 2–3 Tbsp. paprika
- ¾ cup red wine
- 1 cup sour cream

Place seasoned flour in paper bag and shake beef cubes in it, a few at a time, until well coated. Brown meat in heavy kettle with 2 Tbsp. butter. Add more as necessary. Remove beef, drain on paper towels. Add more butter to kettle. Sauté onion, mushrooms, and garlic until tender. Return meat to kettle, season with salt and pepper, savory, and oregano. Sprinkle paprika over surface of meat until red, then stir; redden surface again. Add dry red wine (Burgundy), cover kettle and simmer slowly. Stir occasionally for three hours until meat is fork tender. Add more wine as needed to keep from getting too thick. Just before serving stir in sour cream. Serve over rice or noodles. Serves 15 to 20. Refrigerate any leftovers because it is even better several days later.

Other recipes likely to turn up on her dinner table included vichyssoise, cold tomato soup (canned tomato soup, barely doctored), baked rice with green chilis, French toast Curaçao, and mocha Macadamia cheesecake. These are dishes that might appear on many less elegant dinner tables. Where is the quail on toast points? The escargot?

Electra was, perhaps above all, a lady of surprises and contradictions.

PART III

The Waggoner Legacy

CHAPTER SEVEN

The Surprise Heir

BUCKY WHARTON WAS UNDOUBTEDLY A SURPRISE TO E. PAUL, Gene Willingham, and Electra II, those who considered themselves the rightful heirs to the ranch. They knew about him, of course—he had spent summers and Christmases at the ranch with Buster, his father. But he and Buster were not close, and his claim on Buster's part of the inheritance must have surprised them all. It certainly surprised Bucky.

Buster Wharton died in 1963 at the ranch. He left everything to his current wife, Lula. But his death set off a string of lawsuits from several others who had claim to his part of the inheritance or thought they did. Among them was Bucky, A. B. Wharton III. Bucky, who had been raised in Albuquerque by his mother, Larita Rohla, might not have challenged the will, but his mother was determined to see her son get what she considered his rightful inheritance. He was the only direct descendant of W. T. among the claimants, except for E. Paul, whose claim seemed based on a "what-if" claim to more of W. T.'s legacy.

Other contenders were Buster's widow, Lula, named in the will; Rita Lorena Wharton, Lula's daughter who Buster adopted—she sought half the assets, claiming to be lawful issue and heir; the Guy Waggoner Trust, which claimed that when Guy's son, young Tom Wharton Waggoner, died at age twenty-five, his share of the trust would have reverted to Guy and

E. Paul; Naomi Ruth Wharton, widow of A. B. Wharton and stepmother to Buster—she claimed a fourth of the assets; not to be left out, E. Paul claimed the estate reverted to him.

The case made its slow way through the courts for more than six and a half years, giving gainful employment to more than twenty-five lawyers. E. Paul died before it was decided. The court ruled in favor of Bucky; the Civil Court of Appeals in Amarillo ruled in favor of Bucky; and, finally, the Texas Supreme Court ruled in his favor, too. A. B. Wharton III was the sole heir to half the Waggoner Estate. This set up Electra II and A. B. III as owners of equal shares—neither could outvote the other. John Biggs was the sole trustee at the time.

Bucky was in high school at Culver Military Academy in Indiana when his father died; he earned a degree from the University of the Americas in Mexico City and then was drafted. He was in the army at Fort Bragg, North Carolina, when he got word that he was the heir to an empire he knew little to nothing about. Buster had not passed on any knowledge of cattle or oil to his son—he had only cared about his polo ponies.

In 1970, Bucky moved to the ranch and began what he considered his real education. He worked in the various divisions of the ranch—cattle, oil, and horses—for six months, learning from the ground up. He earned a master's degree in business administration from Midwestern University in Wichita Falls. At first, he lived in an apartment near Zacaweista, the home built by his grandmother, the first Electra. In 1976, he married Joline, whom he knew from Albuquerque, and together they renovated Zacaweista, which, according to him, was in sad shape. It was built at a time when houses were dark, with small windows; maybe the most important change Bucky and Joline made was to put in large windows and open the house up to the ranch views all around it.

From the start, the Biggs half of the ranch treated Bucky like an outsider. Privately, according to Gary Cartwright, they looked down on the Wharton side, considering Buster a spendthrift given to debauchery, despite Electra's earlier friendship with him, and Bucky an outsider. Buster had borrowed money from his grandmother, Ella, to maintain his lifestyle after the enormous cost of buying out Guy's heirs; the indomitable Ella sold the note to E. Paul, which gave the latter leverage over his rival. E. Paul was plotting ways to get Bucky off the ranch.

In the late 1970s, with E. Paul and John Biggs both dead, Killeen Moore became the trustee. He had been schooled by Biggs, and there was no doubt where his loyalty lay. He got rid of anyone friendly to Bucky and, at one point, tried to buy Bucky out, at a cost so cheap it was an insult. Moore openly told Bucky to go back to Arizona because he would never have a voice on the ranch. Moore resigned in the 1980s and was replaced by two men, each of whom resigned because he could not reconcile the two sides and was limited by the conflict. After the second resignation, Bucky and the Biggs faction could not agree on a trustee, and the position remained vacant.

But Bucky had come to love the land and his heritage. He struck a deal with Electra that extended the trust until 2003, with the stipulation either side could terminate with or without cause on any five-year anniversary. In 1990, Bucky notified Electra that he wanted to terminate the trust and divide the ranch in half in 1991. He had spent hours and enlisted professionals to determine a fair way to divide the land, livestock, buildings, and other assets, and he offered her first choice. Her attorneys responded by filing a petition to liquidate the estate and distribute the assets. They contended it would be difficult to divide four sections, scores of cowboy camps, groups of houses, barns, barracks, an airplane and airstrip, feedlots, pipelines, oil wells, and whatever else. Those who knew Electra claimed she cared little for the cattle and the daily operation but loved the ranch and the heritage. It was unlikely that she would suggest selling, and Cartwright suggests that Willingham was trying to call Bucky's bluff.

Bucky and Gene Willingham were polar opposites. Gene was described as a gregarious good ol' boy who adopted the cowboy image; Bucky was quiet and reserved, usually wore jeans and a polo shirt, and never tried to look like a cowboy. The two men were comanaging the ranch and shared adjacent offices at the ranch headquarters building in Vernon, but they never spoke. They communicated by written message; if they had to meet, both made sure others were present. They quarreled over everything. An example: Willingham wanted to sell hunting leases; Bucky objected that hunters were inconsiderate tenants, leaving gates open, scattering trash, and so on. The families did not speak either—Christmas gifts were exchanged but delivered by messenger.

Negotiations were off and on. At one point, it looked like there was a deal to divide the ranch that hung up only over who would maintain the dam on the Santa Rosa lake. The dam sat right on the dividing line. Willingham said he knew an expert to consult, walked out of the room, and never replied or reported. Each side blamed the other side for stalling. Some saw Electra as the last hope for settlement, claiming again that she would never sell the land. But she died during these stalled negotiations.

In 2003, the terms of the trust expired, and the fate of the ranching empire was left up to the courts. When the two sides couldn't agree on a division and it looked inevitable that the courts would order the property sold, Bucky held out for payment in kind—he would take his share of the assets in property. The courts eventually decided against him.

The historic ranch was put on the market in 2015 at a price of $725 million. With it went a family heritage of 165 years and a way of life for many cowboys and their families. Many working cowboys on the ranch were second- and third-generation Waggoner employees. There was a general feeling that working on the Waggoner defined the cowboy way of life, even after the addition of a helicopter to herd cattle. If the ranch sold, the cowboy way of life would die. There were few if any other large ranches where cowboys could work, and yet many of the men knew no other way of life. And their families often lived on the ranch.

At the age of seventy-nine, one cowboy reminisced, "I went to work there when I was thirteen. My daddy was a cowboy there, so I was, too. I started out in 1937 for $35 a week and room and board. . . . It was a good place to work, a lot of good men to work with and a good life. If it weren't, I don't imagine I'd have done it for fifty-three years." Another younger cowboy, confessing that he knew no other way of life, said he tried college in Vernon for a year, but it didn't work out. "I never could live in the city," he said, referring to Vernon with its population of a little over ten thousand.

The town of Vernon, too, was in suspense over the sale. Vernon's economy was inextricably tied to the ranch. It was like having a huge factory complex in the middle of the city, providing steady employment for residents. Calling the Waggoners the "last true Texans," a former cowboy said, "They pretty much owned all the country around Vernon. They took care of the town." And a Vernon attorney who grew up on the ranch mused, "Wouldn't it be a terrible legacy to be the ones who finally lost the Waggoner ranch?"

Stan Kroenke, the new owner, is not a man who talks to the media. His staff generally does not comment either. But when the sale went through, Kroenke issued a statement vowing to protect and preserve the legacy of the Waggoner family. He called it an honor to be able to carry on the traditions. Some in the area worried that the ranch land would be broken up and sold piecemeal to developers. The general manager of the U.S. division of Kroenke ranches set those fears at ease: "Development is not something we do on these ranches."

Three years later, most things still seem okay in Waggoner country. The city manager of Vernon says little has changed and the ranch is still the biggest employer in the area. The city administrator in Electra, Steve Bowlin, says he sees some good coming out of the sale. The State of Texas will create a perimeter around Electra to act as a firewall. Some of this perimeter will be on Waggoner land and marks the first time in many years that a state agency has been allowed on the private property. Not everyone is happy, though.

Two public lakes are within the ranch boundaries—Lake Diversion and the more popular Lake Kemp, which brings tourists to nearby Seymour to enjoy its parks and long shoreline. For decades, people have built homes around both lakes on land they leased from the Waggoner ranch. Many of the homes were renovated mobile homes, a few were built with loving hands, and some were substantial.

In August 2016, some two hundred residents of homes in Cara Blanca Park at Lake Diversion received eviction notices. They were told to vacate by January 31, 2017, taking with them whatever they wanted to save and salvage. After the deadline, they would be considered trespassers. A few lucky tenants were able to move entire houses; others stripped their houses of anything valuable—wood paneling for walls, window and door frames. A few simply walked away from their homes. One woman spray-painted messages of her defiance on the exterior of her stone home before she left.

According to Steve Biedermann, city administrator of Seymour, notices have more recently gone to residents at Lake Kemp. Asked about the effect on tourism for Seymour, he said it was unlikely to be severe since access to the lake was still permitted for a fee. "With the end of the drought, fishing has rebounded," he said, indicating he expects the usual stream of visitors to the lake to continue. "But people are talking about losing homes they've had for years, some as long as fifty years." There were individual hardship stories—people on disability or scraping by on social security with no place else to go, retirees who had sunk life savings into upgrading their homes. At Lake Diversion, one resident committed suicide, rumor said because he was too old and too broke to start over. Former residents feel betrayed by Kroenke and by the Waggoner family, especially for not giving them more than five months to evacuate.

Kroenke indicated he wanted to let the shore at Lake Diversion return to its natural state to improve the ecosystem. Angry residents have suggested he will open the land to hunting, which was never allowed on Waggoner land in the 165-year history of the ranch. One man explained that there were so many deer at Lake Diversion because they knew they were safe there. Few outsiders know about the lake, sometimes called one of Texas's best-kept secrets, which probably accounts for the plentiful wildlife and serenely quiet atmosphere. Other Kroenke ranches do have hunting programs, and there have been rumors of a hunting program being developed at the Three D. However, far from returning the land to its natural state, ranch management has simply abandoned it, so the now-derelict empty houses dot the land. There has been no effort to demolish them, as of September 2019.

Epilogue

It's risky to try to make judgments about past generations, people who are long gone and can't speak for themselves. We know only what history has left us—in newspapers, articles, and books written retrospectively, stodgy court records that always tell an incomplete story, a journal if we're lucky, perhaps photographs.

Unfortunately, the Waggoners were not a family given to introspection—they left no personal record of their inner thoughts, dreams, or desires. Yes, there are those scrapbooks that belonged to Electra II, but they only reveal external reports of what she thought was important, although her choices indicate much about her life. Still, those books are apparently forever locked away from public view.

Despite blaring headlines and flamboyant lifestyles, the Waggoners valued their privacy. It would be easy to say that the pattern of their lives, the feuds and lawsuits that bedeviled them, the path that led to the sale of the ranch if you will, began when W. T. bestowed great wealth, in cash and land, on his children, wealth they had not worked for. In *"Showdown at the Waggoner Ranch,"* Gary Cartwright put it this way: "The family feud began the moment the old man rigged the game." Even W. T. recognized that the bequests had been a mistake when he rescinded them some years later and established that unworkable trust. But that seems a simplistic assessment, even though history has often demonstrated that second and third generations do not live up to the strength and accomplishments of the forefathers. Besides, it's not all true in this case.

An argument might be made that family fortunes changed with a shift in power from men to women, but that at first seems not an argument that speaks well for the women. Daniel Waggoner definitely lived in a man's world—ranching. His work was the masculine work of a nineteenth-century cattleman—building a cattle herd, acquiring land, driving cattle to market, and accumulating wealth. He was good at it and successful. But history tells us little about his wife, Cicily—the only clear independent move on her part that research uncovered was that after Daniel's death, she bought and sold real estate in Fort Worth, including selling a house on Quality Hill. We can surmise her early life, as we did Ella Halsell Waggoner's childhood, from the memoir of their cousin, Harry—*Cowboys and Cattlemen*.

History does not tell us a lot more about Ella, but from bits gathered here and there, we can piece together a picture of a fairly strong-willed woman and an ambitious mother. She once chastised W. T. for not keeping her informed of the latest changes in a building plan in Fort Worth, and it was Ella who arranged for the first Electra to go to an eastern finishing school and then for a European tour. Undoubtedly, the first Electra's life would have been different had she finished her schooling in Decatur and married the local boy. As it was, she became a thrice-married international celebrity whose lifestyle undoubtedly contributed to her early demise.

Electra I, the only female of the third generation, was the dominant figure of the three W. T. Waggoner offspring. She had her father wrapped around her finger, and her brothers paled in comparison, despite wealth, horses, and countless marriages. She became the symbol of the family, attracting headlines from Thistle Hill to Shadowlawn in Dallas, though the headlines seem to have slowed by the time she moved to New York to be near her son. Perhaps ill health curtailed her activities. Still, while Guy went off to New Mexico and E. Paul stayed home with his quarter horses, Electra carried the banner for the family.

In some ways, Electra II combined the strengths and weaknesses of the Waggoner family. Born to wealth and privilege, she seemed to accept it as her due. In my brief encounter with her years ago, I got an impression of imperiousness and a tendency to dominate. In her carefree youth, she was every bit the celebrity and party girl her legendary aunt had been.

But Electra Biggs eschewed the pattern of her uncle and aunt and followed her parents' example—after a brief and unsuccessful early marriage, she married for love and remained married until John Biggs died. Although she traveled widely and often, the ranch was her home base, and she seemed as tied to it as her father was before her.

The Waggoner dedication to success—obsession if you will—came out in her sculpture. Just as W. T. set his goal as the most land and the best cattle and horses, she set hers as the best sculpture. While she may not have achieved worldwide fame, she worked hard to develop her skill and achieve some mastery in her chosen art form. She exhibited the Waggoner drive and deserved admiration.

By 2003, when the trust ran out, Bucky Wharton was the only direct descendent of his generation left. Much of the Waggoner legacy—the strengths and weaknesses—seem to have missed him, perhaps because the family was only a scant influence in his early years. We know little to nothing about his mother's influence on him, only that at the crucial moment she went to battle to defend his rights. So anything said about him is largely conjecture, but it seems that Bucky treated the world fairly and expected it to return the favor. He made a good-faith effort—several of them—to save the ranch, or at least his half of it, but ran up against forces—and people—too tough for him. He was too nice a guy for the likes of the Biggs branch of the family and probably, especially, for Gene Willingham, who, as Gary Cartwright wrote, loved the money.

Electra IV, either divorced or widowed and remarried, lives in an upscale neighborhood in Fort Worth. A public directory lists residences for Helen Willingham in Little Elm and Pampa, both in Texas. Being of the fifth generation, they missed the legal battles, except perhaps tangentially through Willingham's participation. The way the daughters secured their mother's scrapbooks, though, indicates they would be unlikely to comment today.

Buck Wharton (he apparently does not go by Bucky, though that is how he is referred to in every source I found) wrote a gracious note, saying he and his family loved the ranch and felt blessed to have lived a great portion of their lives there. Now, he would like to leave it in the past as something positive rather than digging around in memories to uncover something they would just as soon not have to deal with. He makes his home in a Fort Worth suburb.

For most of his life, Buck was estranged from those who probably considered themselves the core of the Waggoner family—born too late to know the grandmother who gave him Waggoner status; distanced as a child by geography, with occasional visits to his father; distanced as an adult by lawsuits and an almost openly hostile reception. Yet he was the one who followed the dream of the most land, the best cattle.

Vernon, Electra, and Seymour—Texas Towns Impacted by the Waggoner Ranch

A wide swath of central North Texas is economically impacted by—and to some extent dependent on—the Waggoner Ranch, but three communities are almost contingent with ranch land. They are the city of Vernon and the smaller towns of Electra and Seymour.

Vernon, slightly north of the ranch and almost but not quite on the western edge, is one of the larger of the communities that dot Highway 287 between Wichita Falls and Amarillo. It is the seat of Wilbarger County and has a population that consistently hovers around ten thousand to twelve thousand. Numbers of settlers came to the area after the Civil War, and the post office was established in 1889. The name *Vernon* was probably a tribute to George Washington's Mount Vernon, though some stories claim that there was a traveling whisky salesman named Vernon Brown in the region at that time. The railroad arrived in 1885.

Today, Vernon is a center for agriculture-related products and oil. It is the home of the Waggoner Ranch offices, Vernon College, and the Red River Valley Museum. The college, opened in 1972 with 608 students, offers an associate degree in a variety of academic and tech-related vocational subjects. Today, the enrollment is right at three thousand with fifty-some faculty members.

Housed on the campus of the college, the Red River Valley Museum has three main collections—the Berry collection of fossils and artifacts from the area, the Bill Bond collection of 135 game mounts representing animals from the Arctic Circle to Africa, and the Waggoner Gallery, which features the history of the Waggoner Ranch, sculptures, a replica of Electra Biggs's studio, and a large mural by Adrian Martinez depicting the ranch history. In other exhibits, an animatronic cowboy recounts the history of the nearby Great Western Trail and tribute is paid to musicians Roy Orbison and Jack Teagarden, who had roots in Vernon.

Electra, Texas, is also on Highway 287, fifteen miles northwest of Wichita Falls and slightly northeast of one corner of the ranch. The Waggoners figure prominently in the town's history, as the town's name suggests. Electra is also where W. T. accidentally discovered oil while drilling for water. In 1905, the Waggoners sold their land, and the Electra Land and Colonization Company was formally laid out in streets and plots. Despite repeated efforts to attract residents, the population remains around three thousand. The town is in Wichita County.

Seymour, seat of Baylor County, is south of the ranch's southern border. It was established with a post office in 1879 and probably named after a local cowboy. In its early years, Seymour saw sometimes-violent clashes between cowboys and settlers, but order was eventually restored. Today the town is an agribusiness and legal center, with some small manufacturing. The population is around three thousand.

Seymour has two tourist draws—the annual Old Settlers Reunion and Rodeo and Lake Kemp, eight miles north, which offers recreational opportunities in parks and a hundred miles of shoreline.

Further Reading

The 2015 listing of the Waggoner Ranch for sale prompted several videos that provide a good overview and introduction to the ranch and its divisions—oil, cattle, horses. The cinematography is good, the landscape spectacular—and it makes you wonder, as one observer said, about being the one who broke up the dynasty. An internet search for "YouTube sale Waggoner Ranch" will turn up several choices. The best video runs about six minutes.

Two thick books by the late Roze McCoy Porter are devoted to the Waggoners. The first, *Thistle Hill: The Cattle Baron's Legacy* (Branch-Smith Inc., 1980), purportedly deals with the first Electra and her magnificent Fort Worth mansion, but Porter managed to work in the history of the ranch and a lot of tangential material. The second book is *Electra II,* a title that accurately describes the focus of the study, although it repeats material from the first. The first volume is not indexed but does have a bibliography. They are not particularly good books. One suspects they were written with the "helpful collaboration" of Electra II and for her approval, for they are extended puff pieces where every gown is elegant, every home magnificent, every man handsome. Among other problems, Porter was loose with dates and place names. In the first book she dates Electra's opening at the Seligmann Galleries in 1934; in the second, it is more believably in 1938. Similarly, of Guy Waggoner's move to New Mexico, Porter sends him to the Bell Ranch in *Thistle Hill*, while in the second book he goes to the Mosquero Ranch, more believable since Mosquero is the county seat near the property. One suspects Electra drew dates and names out of distant memory, and Porter failed to check them.

However, Porter's books are like Wikipedia—a good starting place, and if one doesn't look to them for accuracy, they give a pretty good outline of the story of the Waggoner heritage.

Other helpful books include C. L. Douglas's *Cattle Kings of Texas* (State House Press, 1989). It is a compilation of articles, including one about Dan and W. T. Waggoner, published in *The Cattleman Magazine*, 1925–1937, and subsequently published as a book. *The Cattleman* republished a posthumous edition in 1989.

The late Jerry Flemmons, a journalist and longtime columnist for the *Fort Worth Star-Telegram*, wrote an entertaining and realistic biography of the newspaper's legendary owner, Amon G. Carter. The Waggoners are mentioned, including the wonderful story of the "statue caper," early attempts to unbox Electra's statue of Will Rogers. A first edition of *Amon: The Life of Amon Carter, Sr. of Texas* (Jenkins Publishing Company, 1978) is hard to find, but an abridged and less entertaining version has since been published. The second version was issued after a member of Carter's family objected to the myth-breaking honesty of Flemmons's original text.

Harry Halsell, Ella Waggoner's cousin, got into the memoir business with *Cowboys and Cattleland*. (Borodino Books, 2017). First published in 1937, the book is one of several published versions. One edition, sanctioned by the author's daughter, internationally known journalist Grace Halsell, was published in 2000 by TCU Press. The Borodino edition is available as a reasonably priced eBook. It recounts episodes from life on the prairie and the years of Indian depredations and therefore provides interesting background for the life of Ella Halsell Waggoner.

Brenda McClurkin worked with Historic Fort Worth Inc. to produce *Fort Worth's Quality Hill,* (Arcadia Publishing, 2014). It details the Waggoner family's move to Fort Worth and includes some rare photographs of Thistle Hill and a good overview of the wealthy cattle baron mansion. In addition, this author's monograph, *Thistle Hill: The History and the House* (TCU Press, 1988), gives both historical and architectural information, although ongoing renovation has rendered some of the architectural information out of date.

Dining with the Cattle Barons (Texian Press, 1981) by Sarah Morgan provides incidental information by focusing on the food on the big ranches and includes one of the second Electra's favorite entertaining recipes, included in this book.

Ann Drake apparently self-published "an interpretive history" of the life of Daniel Waggoner. Called *Clear Fork Kinship* (A. N. Drake Publishing, 2008), it is listed at $145 on Amazon, with a used copy as high as $223.

Noted Texas journalists have turned their attention to the Waggoners from time to time. One of the most helpful sources I found was Gary Cartwright's "Showdown at the Waggoner Ranch" (*Texas Monthly,* January 2004). Also helpful were "The Storied Waggoners Are a Story unto Themselves," by Joe Holley (*Houston Chronicle Native Texans,* September 20, 2014, updated May 21, 2015) and "Mammoth Estate to Be Split Up, Auctioned," by Evan Moore (*Houston Chronicle,* July 27, 2003).

As always when researching Texas subjects, *Handbook of Texas Online* (Texas State Historical Association) was invaluable. Not only does it provide information on everyone from Dan Waggoner to Electra Waggoner Wharton, but also the sources listed for each article offer interesting trails to follow.

One advantage of notoriety or flamboyance is that the newspapers pay attention. The online databases of the *Fort Worth Star-Telegram* and the *Dallas Morning News* after 1900 were of particular help. A more contemporary source were occasional columns, "Hometown by Handlebars" from Mike Nichols in the *Star-Telegram*.

For insights into the effect of the sale of the Waggoner Ranch, see Trish Choate, "Waggoner Ranch Sale Jolts Land-holders" (*Wichita Falls Times Record News*, February 25, 2018), and Leif Reigistad, "Cast Out of Eden" (*Texas Monthly*, March 2017).

For those who might want to put the Waggoner women in the context of other Texas ranch women, a reading list might include the following: Carmen Goldthwaite, *Texas Ranch Women*; Helen Kleberg Groves, *Bob and Helen Kleberg of the King Ranch*; Hallie Stillwell, *I'll Gather My Geese*; Mamie Sypert Burns, *This I Can Leave You, a Woman's Days on the Pitchfork Ranch*; and Jane Clements Monday and Frances Brannen Vick, *Letters to Alice: Birth of the Kleberg-King Ranch Dynasty*.

About the Author

Judy Alter is the author of over a hundred books—fiction and nonfiction for both adults and young adults. Her awards include the 2005 Owen Wister Award for Lifetime Achievement, Spur Awards from Western Writers of America for the novel *Mattie* and the short story "Sue Ellen Learns to Dance," Western Heritage (Wrangler) Awards for "Sue Ellen Learns to Dance" and "Fool Girl," and a Best Juvenile of the Year Award from the Texas Institute of Letters for *Luke and the Van Zandt County War*. She was named one of the Outstanding Women of Fort Worth by the Mayor's Commission on the Status of Women in 1989 and was listed by *Dallas Morning News* (March 10, 1999) as one of one hundred women, past and present, who made their mark on Texas. She has been inducted into the Western Writers of America Hall of Fame and the Texas Literary Hall of Fame.